CONTENTS

MONEY

MONEY

REPORT #1

THE ECONOMIC "CRYSTAL BALL" WALL STREET INSIDERS SWEAR BY

Source: **Lakshman Achuthan,** managing director of Economic Cycle Research Institute (ECRI), a research firm in New York City that uses economic indexes to forecast booms and busts. He is coauthor, with Anirvan Banerji, ECRI's research director, of *Beating the Business Cycle* (Doubleday).

Wouldn't it be great if every time you were about to embark on a major financial decision you could consult your crystal ball about what was likely to happen in the broader economy? Of course, there is no such thing—but one indicator comes close.

When the economy still appeared robust in September of 2000, forecaster Lakshman Achuthan's "Economic Dashboard" warned of the impending recession. Within six months, the prediction had come true.

Achuthan was asked about the forecasting techniques he used to make that prescient call and what his indicator is predicting now...

When you talk about an Economic Dashboard, what exactly do you mean?

Our Dashboard is made up of three leading indexes—the Weekly Leading Index, the Leading Home Price Index and the Future Inflation Gauge. When the information is combined, they do a good job of forecasting turns in the economy, inflation and home prices.

Each index has many components. For example, the Weekly Leading Index includes seven indicators that were chosen based on their track records over the past 80 years.

Each of the Weekly Leading Index components is published either daily or weekly. The Dashboard as a whole has correctly predicted each of the last two recessions without giving false signals of recessions that never occurred. While the index was introduced in the early 1980s, based on back testing, it would have predicted every recession since 1948.

How much notice of turns in the economy does your system actually provide?

The Weekly Leading Index will start indicating a turn in the economy eight to nine months before it occurs. To avoid false alarms, it's best to wait two months before considering a signal of impending change significant. That means the effective lead time is six months.

In our last recession call, the Weekly Leading Index began to signal a change in the economy early in 2000. We were virtually alone in September of that year when we went public with our recession warning. Even when the recession had already begun in March 2001, 95% of American economists still thought there wouldn't be a recession.

Sometimes it goes against human nature to trust the Weekly Leading Index—especially because a signal is likely to come when nine out of 10 of your colleagues think that no change is at hand.

How can we put your Economic Dashboard to practical use?

Use it as a guide whenever you have to make a significant financial decision, the outcome of which could be affected by a change in the economy. For instance, it could be enormously helpful to know whether demand for whatever you are buying will hit a peak or a low in the near future.

Say you are in the market for a home and you have some flexibility about when you can buy. If the Weekly Leading Index points to continued strength for the economy, you might delay the purchase until the index points to a slowdown. At that point, home prices likely will have softened. Conversely, as a home seller, you might speed up the transaction if the economy is heading toward recession and home prices appear likely to fall.

Also check the component of the Dashboard that focuses on real estate—the Leading Home Price Index. Even though many experts expected home prices to fall in the wake of the recession, the Home Price Index kept increasing—pointing to higher home prices and no housing bubble bursting (yet).

Can your Economic Dashboard forecast the stock market?

Actually, it's the other way around. The stock market is an indicator for the economy. It is one of the seven economic indicators that make up our Weekly Leading Index. It's not the best indicator because the stock market sometimes will decline sharply without the economy falling into recession.

Still, the stock market's performance is one of the key indicators. If it declines along with the other components of the Weekly Leading Index, then it's signaling recession. The stock market peaked early in 2000—months before we made our recession call and a year before the recession officially began.

That's a long lead time. What would waiting for your last recession warning have done for my stock portfolio?

Selling stocks in response to our recession warning in September 2000 would have allowed you to step aside for the bulk of the bear market and then get back in again before the rally began.

You wouldn't have gotten out at the market's peak, but you would have gotten out early enough to have protected most of your gains. The Dow was down by only 8% from its peak on January 14, 2000. By the time it bottomed on October 9, 2002, it had lost a total of 38%. For the S&P 500 Index, the loss was 49% from its high on March 24, 2000, to its low on October 9, 2002.

By the way, the index would have started guiding people back into the market early in 2002, about six months before stocks hit bottom. This isn't "perfect" timing, but you would have had the opportunity to purchase stocks at or close to their lows.

Is there an easy way to follow your research?

Sure. The Weekly Leading Index is updated at 10:30 am every Friday on our Web site, *www.businesscycle.com.* You can view it for free—additional research is available to subscribers for a charge. Free articles from Reuters (*http://today. reuters.com/news/home.aspx*) interpreting the updated index numbers also are available on our site.

Investor's Business Daily usually runs an article on the index in its Saturday edition.

Also, an Economic Cycle Research Institute researcher appears on TV's CNBC business channel at 11 am (ET) the day the monthly employment report is released.

■

REPORT #2

REFUSE TO LOSE IN THE STOCK MARKET

Source: **Christopher Cordaro, CFA, CFP,** RegentAtlantic Capital LLC, Chatham, NJ, *www.regentatlantic.com.*

Consider the following example…if a stock is priced at $100/share, buy *put options* that give you the right to sell the stock at $90/share within 12 or 24 months. Then sell *call options*, which let someone else have the right to buy your stock at $120/share over the same period. This structure is called a *collar.*

The cost of the put and the proceeds from the call should be equal to limit your downside and ensure you get at least $90 a share. If the stock price falls below $90, you still can sell it for $90. If it rises above $120, you can sell it or buy back the call option.

CAUTION: Options trading is complex—consult a knowledgeable financial adviser.

■

REPORT #3

HOW TO GET GUARANTEED PROTECTION FOR YOUR NEST EGG

Source: Money, Time-Life Bldg., Rockefeller Center, New York City 10020.

Get FDIC insurance for CDs worth as much as $20 million without having to open 200 separate accounts of $100,000 each—the maximum insured per account by the FDIC. Use the Certificate of Deposit Account Registry Service (CDARS), that is offered by a growing network of banks. Through CDARS, your money appears in a single account but it is actually spread out among multiple accounts by the bank, so that it's fully insured. CDARS rates often are higher than those for standard CDs.

INFORMATION: 866-776-6426, *www.cdars.com.*

■

REPORT #4

OUR FAVORITE MONEY SECRETS

BUYING STOCKS COMMISSION-FREE...

The number of dividend reinvestment plans (DRIPs) that allow investors to make initial stock purchases directly has tripled since 1997. There now are about 600 plans from US and foreign companies...and more of them than ever are open to those who are not yet shareholders.

HELPFUL: *www.dripinvestor.com* and *www.sharebuilder.com.*

*Source: **Charles B. Carlson, CFA,** editor, DRIP Investor, 7412 Calumet Ave., Hammond, IN 46324.*

CASHING IN...

Get cash for life insurance with a *life settlement.* Even policies with no cash value, such as term policies, may have value in life settlements. *Viatical settlements* are used when the insured is terminally or chronically ill.

EXAMPLE: Someone who took out a policy at age 60 and now is 72, has had a stroke and has heart disease, and can no longer afford policy premiums. Sale proceeds are not taxable. *Senior settlements* are used for anyone over age 65 who no longer needs his/her policy. Tax may be due on a portion of the proceeds. Life-settlement investors are interested in policies with face values of $250,000 or more. They might pay 10% to 30% of face value. Consult your financial adviser or attorney.

Source: **Keith Wegen,** vice president of finance, American Wealth Transfer Group LLP, Boulder, CO.

PAY FOR COLLEGE WITH FREQUENT-FLIER MILES...

The *BabyMint* college-savings program is just one of several buyer-reward programs, such as *Upromise,* that credit a portion of purchases from certain retailers to a college-savings account, such as a 529 plan. BabyMint also allows airline miles from certain carriers—Alaska, Delta, Midwest and US Airways —to be exchanged for cash contributions to participants' college-funding accounts.

INFORMATION: BabyMint, 888-427-1099, *www.babymint.com.*

WAIT UNTIL JUNE TO BUY ELECTRONICS...

Retailers clear out inventory to make room for newly up-graded equipment in January and June. Prices of older models typically fall by 10% or more.

CAUTION: Before buying, find out what new features are about to come to market. If they are ones you care about, buying an older model may not be a bargain after all.

Source: Money, Time-Life Bldg., Rockefeller Center, New York City 10020.

WARRANTY WISDOM...

Extended warranties seldom make sense, even for big-ticket items. Warranties for appliances are least worthwhile because most appliances are now very reliable. Extended warranties only make sense for plasma TVs, laptop PCs and treadmills and elliptical trainers with warranties of less than one year.

Source: Consumer Reports, 101 Truman Ave., Yonkers, NY 10703.

REPORT #5

SAVE 30% ON HEATING OIL THIS WINTER

Source: **Bill Keith,** a home-remodeling contractor for 25 years in St. John, IN, and now host of *The Home Tips Show* on Chicago-area PBS-TV and radio stations. His Web site is *www.billkeith.com.*

Heating and air-conditioning ducts that are leaky can increase utility bills by as much as 30%. For about $300, an energy consultant can do a pressure test to locate leaks. For an additional cost, he/she can seal them.

TO FIND A CONSULTANT: Ask your gas or electric company... call a reputable insulation contractor...get in touch with the department of energy in your state.

CAUTION: Always check references before hiring anyone.

REPORT #6

HOW TO CASH IN BIG AS OIL PRICES SOAR

Source: **Stephen Leeb, PhD,** president of Leeb Capital Management, a money-management firm based in New York City, *www.leeb.net.* He is coauthor of *The Oil Factor: Protect Yourself—and Profit—from the Coming Energy Crisis* (Warner).

The days of cheap gas are gone for good. Soon, even $3.50 per gallon might seem like a bargain. During this decade, Americans could be paying more than $5 a gallon for gasoline. Heating oil prices will likely double or triple.

We have had oil crises before—adjusting for inflation, gasoline reached nearly $3 a gallon in March 1981—yet prices always returned to "normal."

Why should this time be different? In the past, skyrocketing oil prices were caused by OPEC embargoes or Middle Eastern political instability. But this time, the central issue is a supply-demand imbalance that will only get worse.

As oil prices rise, our lives could change dramatically, resulting in challenges and investment opportunities...

SUPPLY CRUNCH...

Oil demand is soaring, thanks in large part to the improving world economy—China's in particular. The US Department of Energy estimates that world demand will grow by 50% in the next two decades.

Supply can't keep pace. OPEC already is near 100% production capacity. Middle Eastern nations have not added significant new production facilities in 25 years, and they are unlikely to do so anytime soon. Oil capacity in the continental US and in the North Sea region, which includes Norway, Denmark and the UK, is well past its peak.

INVESTMENT OPPORTUNITY: Schlumberger Limited is a leader in oil-field-discovery technology. That skill will be increasingly useful as oil prices rise and locating even small untapped reserves becomes more profitable.

DRIVING IMPACT...

The typical American vehicle gets 24 miles per gallon and is driven approximately 12,000 miles per year. When gas went for $1 a gallon, the annual expense was $500. At $3 a gallon, we have to ante up another $1,000. At $5 a gallon, the average American will have to pay $2,500 per year. That should persuade most of us to buy more fuel-efficient vehicles. This might be a smart time to trade in your sport-utility vehicle (SUV) for a smaller ride. If you wait just a few years, a large vehicle's resale value will likely suffer.

INVESTMENT OPPORTUNITY: Toyota Motor is a world leader in the design and marketing of small, fuel-efficient vehicles. It also has a better balance sheet than most major automakers.

ALTERNATIVE FUELS...

Higher oil prices will heighten development of alternative fuels. The most economical of the environmentally friendly options is wind power. Nuclear energy, solar power and coal also could get renewed attention.

INVESTMENT OPPORTUNITY: FPL Group, Inc. This Florida-based energy company is the leading US player in wind power.

HOUSING...

The average oil-heated home in the Northeast consumes about 1,500 gallons of oil per year. Large or poorly insulated homes can consume more. At $2.40 per gallon, that's $3,600 a year. Each $1 per gallon increase tacks another $1,500 onto a family's annual heating bill. Natural gas prices have been rising even faster than oil prices.

Owning a larger-than-average home, especially in a cold climate, could become less desirable. The high cost of heating could accelerate the current population shift away from the North. The effect of the price of oil on cooling bills is less direct. There are many other sources of electricity—hydro, coal, wind and nuclear power.

Cities might gain favor—people who live in cities don't pay directly for fuel to commute to work or find entertainment.

SHOPPING...

Higher oil prices will increase the price of virtually everything we buy. Businesses pass along to consumers the higher costs of manufacturing and transporting their goods to stores. Production of plastics, chemicals and pharmaceuticals requires significant amounts of petroleum (derived from oil). Food prices will also increase since petroleum is a key fertilizer component.

INVESTMENT OPPORTUNITY: Treasury inflation-protected securities (TIPS) offer the security of Treasury bonds with built-in protection against inflation. Five-, 10- and 20-year bonds are available. They can be purchased from the Treasury Department (800-722-2678, *www.publicdebt.treas.gov/sec/sectrdir.htm*).

For tax reasons, TIPS are best held in retirement accounts.

ENTERTAINMENT...

When gas prices went through the roof in the 1970s, Americans spent more free time at home watching TV. Now, with the Internet, satellite TV and DVDs, staying at home is even more appealing.

INVESTMENT OPPORTUNITY: Electronic Arts, Inc. Video games are a quintessential stay-at-home form of entertainment, and Electronic Arts is the dominant player in the field. These games are becoming increasingly popular with adults, as those born in the 1980s come of age.

SECTORS TO AVOID...

AIRLINES AND MOST AUTOMAKERS: Earnings will be hurt by rising oil prices.

THE SO-CALLED DEFENSIVE STOCKS (RETAIL STORES, FOOD, HOUSEHOLD PRODUCTS): These companies trade at premium price-to-earnings multiples and have low growth rates. Over the long term, they will have trouble increasing profits to keep up with inflation.

■

REPORT #7

TURN YOUR JUNK INTO CASH

Source: **Adriane G. Berg, elder law attorney,** Morristown, NJ, and New York City, and a founder of the National Academy of Elder Law Attorneys. She is author of 13 books on personal finance, most recently, *How Not to Go Broke at 102! Achieving Everlasting Wealth* (Wiley). She is a national keynote speaker for *USA Today's* retirement seminars. Her Web site is *www.adrianeberg.com.*

Whether you are downsizing after the kids have moved out or you just inherited a house full of antiques, here are the best ways to sell items that you don't need or want— and for a tidy sum...

CONSIGNMENT SHOPS...

Wares typically include clothing, furs, china, collectibles and furniture. The owner of the shop establishes the price. You pay no penalty if your items fail to sell, but they may not be sold for months. You can expect to receive approximately 50% of the sale price.

Smart selling strategies...

• *Choose a shop in an upscale neighborhood to get the highest possible price.*

• *Be sure to get price estimates from several shops*—figures can vary widely.

ESTATE SALES/GARAGE SALES...

These are best for less expensive possessions that you want to sell quickly.

Smart selling strategies...

• *Advertise the sale in the newspaper.*

- *Restrict the sale to certain areas in your house.* Keep more valuable items in a glass case or locked cabinet. Shoplifters frequent estate sales.
- *Expect to haggle.* Most buyers will offer 20% less than your asking price but eventually will compromise at 10% less than your asking price.
- *Hire a professional estate or tag sale organizer if you have many high-quality possessions.* They have large mail and e-mail lists that will attract active buyers. They also can advise you objectively on how to price items and will handle any haggling. Expect to keep 75% of the proceeds. To find an organizer for your sale, check The National Association of Professional Organizers, 847-375-4746, *www.napo.net.*

INTERNET AUCTIONS...

These Web sites are great for disposing of specialized items or small items—appliances, clothing, sporting goods and computer equipment—that wouldn't fetch much at a garage sale.

On-line auctions require time and/or effort—you must photograph items, write descriptions and ship them to buyers—but costs are reasonable. At *www.eBay.com*, the most popular site, you pay a small fee to list items and a percentage of the closing price if they sell. Visit the eBay Web site for complete details.

WORTHWHILE READING: *How to Sell Anything on eBay...*and *Make a Fortune!* by Dennis Prince (McGraw-Hill).

Smart selling strategies...

- *Make sure your auction begins and ends on a weekend—* when on-line activity is brisk.

If you have many items to sell and need storage space, try Portable On Demand Storage (PODS), which, unlike other storage centers, will deliver storage containers directly to your home. You fill the containers, and they are then taken to a local climate-controlled facility that you can access.

COST: $160 per month for rental of an 8' x 8' x 12' container, large enough to hold the contents of a 1,200-square-foot home, plus about $200 for initial delivery and final pickup of the container.

FOR INFORMATION AND TO SEE IF THIS SERVICE IS AVAILABLE IN YOUR AREA: 888-776-7637, *www.podsusa.com.*

AUCTION HOUSES...

These are good for selling valuable antiques, art and jewelry with little effort. The price you pay for ease of sale is the extra cost and wasted time if the item doesn't sell. You're more likely to attract an auction house's interest if you have many valuable items instead of one or two trinkets. An auction representative will appraise the items in your home and transport them to the auction house. After fees and commissions, you will wind up with approximately 50% to 75% of the sale price.

MAJOR AUCTION HOUSES INCLUDE: Bonhams & Butterfields (*www.butterfields.com*)...Christie's (*www.christies.com*)...and Doyle New York (*www.doylenewyork.com*).

Smart selling strategies...

• *Do your own research.* Few people realize that auction houses can be persuaded to increase their appraisals. How to convince them? Prove that similar items recently have been auctioned for higher prices. If, for instance, you have a 19th-century cherry desk, call around and find another auction house that has sold one and ask for a catalog.

COST: $10 to $50 or more per catalog.

ALSO HELPFUL: *Antiques Roadshow Primer* by Carol Prisant and Chris Jussel and *Antiques Roadshow Collectibles* by Carol Prisant (both from Workman). *Kovels' Know Your Collectibles* and *Kovels' Know Your Antiques, Revised and Updated* (both from Random House).

• *Negotiate fees.* Auction houses may reduce or eliminate charges, depending on how badly they want the items you are offering them.

TYPICAL FEES: A hefty charge for placing a photo in the catalog...*a reserve penalty*—you're given a price range and must agree to accept the lowest bid in that range—the reserve. If the item's price doesn't match or exceed the *reserve,* you will be charged 5% of the reserve as a penalty. You also can set your own reserve.

• *Check your insurance coverage.* Most homeowners' policies cover your items while they're at the auction house. Otherwise, you'll pay 2% of the value for temporary insurance.

■

REPORT #8

HOW TO GET FREE (OR ALMOST FREE) PRESCRIPTION DRUGS

Source: **Jim Miller,** writer/creator of "Savvy Senior," a syndicated newspaper question-and-answer column for senior citizens, Norman, OK, *www.savvysenior.org.* He is author of the book *The Savvy Senior* (Hyperion).

Controversial? Definitely. Political? Absolutely. Beneficial? Maybe. The new prescription benefit passed into law in 2003 is the biggest change to Medicare since it began covering health care for elderly and disabled Americans in 1965.

BAD NEWS: Under the drug benefit program, most seniors will save only a modest amount.

GOOD NEWS: People age 64 and younger can now put away money tax-free for their health-care expenses using special new savings accounts.

Here is a look at the Medicare changes...

HEALTH SAVINGS ACCOUNTS...

Many people reduce health insurance costs by buying policies that have high deductibles. The law permits tax-sheltered savings accounts to finance these deductibles—at least $1,050 a year for individuals, $2,100 for couples in 2006. You can receive a tax deduction for contributions, invest this money and pay no taxes on the earnings upon withdrawal, provided the money is used for health expenses, including long-term-care services. Otherwise, a 10% penalty applies.

NEW DRUG PLAN...

More than 10 million of the 42 million Americans covered by Medicare currently have drug coverage, mostly through a former employer. The new drug benefit, called Medicare Part D, will increase those numbers. However, this plan does not make sense for everyone.

It gives the biggest savings to those with low incomes who don't receive Medicaid and those who spend heavily on prescriptions. If you enroll in the plan, you cannot buy supplemental Medicare (Medigap) to help defray drug costs.

DRUG COST...

AMT. SPENT/YR.	YOU PAY...*	YOU SAVE...	
$1,000	$857.50	$142.50	(14%)
$1,500	$982.50	$517.50	(35%)
$2,000	$1,107.50	$892.50	(45%)
$2,500	$1,420.00	$1,080.00	(43%)
$3,000	$1,920.00	$1,080.00	(36%)
$5,000	$3,920.00	$1,080.00	(22%)
$10,000	$4,265.00	$5,735.00	(57%)

WHAT TO DO: Add up your annual drug costs. If you spend less than $810 a year on drugs, it probably doesn't pay to participate. You will spend more on the premium ($420), the deductible ($250) and out-of-pocket medication costs than you will get back. But if you enroll more than three months after your 65th birthday, when you become eligible for Medicare, you are subject to a penalty (1% per month for each month you delay enrollment.) **COST BREAKDOWN...**

• *Premiums.* Generally $35 monthly ($420 per person per year), but they may be higher in certain parts of the US.

• *Deductibles.* There is a $250 deductible for prescription drugs per year.

• *Out-of-pocket charges.* After the deductible, Medicare covers 75% of drug costs up to $2,250.

• *Coverage gap.* For amounts exceeding $2,250 ($750 out-of-pocket**), Medicare will pay nothing until you reach $5,100 ($3,600 out-of-pocket).

• *Catastrophic coverage.* When costs exceed $5,100 ($3,600 out-of-pocket) not including the $420 yearly premium, Medicare pays for 95% of each prescription. Members are responsible for the remaining 5%.

• *Low-income subsidy.* People eligible for Medicaid pay no premium or deductible and have no gap in coverage. They pay $1 per prescription for generics and $3 for brand names. Co-payments are waived for all those in nursing homes, regardless of income. Other benefits are available on a sliding scale to families with incomes below the federal poverty line, depending on assets.

*Total out-of-pocket expenses, including $420 annual premium, $250 deductible and 25% of additional costs based on a complex formula.

**($2,250-250) x 25% plus $250 deductible.

For more information on the drug plan, contact Medicare, 800-MEDICARE, *www.medicare.gov.*

Other changes...

• *Medicare Part B.* While Part A covers hospital care, Part B insurance helps pay for doctors' services and outpatient hospital and emergency room services.

• Premiums. Premiums for doctors' services and outpatient care are higher for people who have annual incomes over $80,000. The premium increases with income, roughly tripling for people with incomes of more than $200,000.

• Deductibles. They will rise from $124 in 2006, increasing by a small percentage each year thereafter.

• Expanded medical coverage. Medicare will cover an initial physical examination for new beneficiaries and screening for diabetes and cardiovascular disease. It will also provide coordinated care for people with chronic illnesses and increase payments for doctors administering mammograms.

• *Private health plans.* The government is offering $12 billion in subsidies to entice private insurers to offer basic health insurance through the Medicare system. INCLUDED IN THESE PLANS ARE THE FOLLOWING...

• Preferred provider organizations (PPOs), which encourage use of in-network doctors but allow patients to go outside the network if they pay extra.

• Private fee-for-service plans, which allow patients to see any doctor.

• *Employer incentives.* Tax breaks worth more than $70 billion over 10 years are provided to employers who maintain drug coverage for retirees. If you already have retiree medical coverage, ask your former employer for a letter stating that its coverage is "creditable coverage" if you do not automatically receive such a statement. This will protect you from a Medicare penalty if you later decide to enroll in Part D.

• *Drugs from Canada.* The law allows drugs to be imported from Canada if the Department of Health and Human Services certifies their safety. So far, the department has refused to do so.

Prescription drugs sold in Canada are 10% to 50% cheaper than comparable drugs sold in the US.

■

REPORT #9

NEVER PAY FULL PRICE FOR MEDICINE AGAIN

Source: **Marvin D. Shepherd, PhD,** director of the Center for Pharmacoeconomic Studies and professor and chair of the Pharmacy Administration Division at the College of Pharmacy, University of Texas, Austin.

Although the increasing costs of drug development continue to drive drug costs up, most people can save *at least* 50%.

SECRET: Smart shopping, plus inside information on how to get the most medication for your money.

Whether you pay for drugs out-of-pocket or have drug coverage, here's the top money-saving advice...

PRICE SHOP...

Prescription drug prices can vary by 25% or more from one pharmacy to the next. Don't assume that big chains have the best prices. Some smaller pharmacies scout out the cheapest drug wholesalers and pass the savings to consumers.

SMART IDEA: Price shop by phone. Call in the evening or weekday afternoons when pharmacists are typically less busy.

BUY ON-LINE...

You can save anywhere from 20% to 50% buying drugs from on-line pharmacies, which have low overhead costs. It's a smart strategy for patients with chronic conditions, such as arthritis or high cholesterol, who use large quantities of the same drugs over time.

For computer users, the most reliable on-line pharmacies include Medco, *www.medco.com*, and Drugstore.com, *www.drugstore.com*.

IMPORTANT: Buy only from on-line pharmacies that display the Verified Internet Pharmacy Provider Site (VIPPS) seal. This means that the company has been inspected and accredited by the National Association of the Boards of Pharmacy. Also, avoid on-line pharmacies that don't require a prescription. This is a sign that the company may be foreign or sells drugs illegally.

REQUEST OLDER DRUGS...

Doctors don't admit it, but they're just as likely as patients to be influenced by slick drug marketing campaigns. Studies have shown that doctors are more likely to prescribe new drugs than older ones—even when there's clear evidence that the older drugs are just as effective and much less expensive.

EXAMPLE: Millions of Americans with osteoarthritis switched to Cox-2 inhibitors, such as *celecoxib* (Celebrex), when these drugs were introduced. For most patients, Cox-2 inhibitors are no more effective than aspirin, acetaminophen or ibuprofen. Now studies show that these drugs may even increase risk for heart attack or stroke. What's more, a single dose of a Cox-2 inhibitor might cost more than $2, compared with pennies for aspirin.

SMART IDEA: Ask your doctor to write prescriptions for older, less-expensive drugs unless there's a compelling medical reason to take a newer medication.

GENERIC DRUGS...

The average price of a brand-name prescription for 2005 was $101.71, compared with $29.82 for a generic, according to the National Association of Chain Drug Stores.

If your doctor prescribes a specific brand-name drug, your pharmacist is permitted under state law to substitute a less-expensive generic.

TO FIND OUT IF A GENERIC IS AVAILABLE: Go to the FDA's Web site, *www.fda.gov/cder/ob/default.htm*, for a list of all FDA-approved drugs and generic equivalents. Or use a drug reference book, such as the *Physicians' Desk Reference* (Thomson) or *The Pill Book* (Bantam), available in bookstores and libraries.

NEW MEDICARE DRUG COVERAGE...

Everyone with Medicare coverage is now eligible to join a Medicare prescription drug plan and get insurance, which covers both brand-name and generic prescription drugs. For more information, visit the Medicare Web site at *www.medicare.gov* or call them at 800-MEDICARE.

BUY IN BULK...

Check with your insurance plan to see if you can get a 90-day supply of your medications. You may be able to save the co-pay charges and dispensing fee charges.

CAUTION: Buy drugs in bulk only if you've already been taking them and know they work for you.

SPLIT PILLS...

You can double the quantity of the doses in a single prescription by getting a higher-strength tablet and using a pill splitter to cut the pills into halves. A 100-milligram (mg) tablet often costs about the same as a 50-mg tablet of the same drug.

IMPORTANT: Capsules cannot be split. Pills that have enteric coatings or other time-release mechanisms also should not be split. Ask your doctor or pharmacist if the pills that you take can be split.

Do *not* use a kitchen knife to split your pills. Use a pill splitter, sold in pharmacies for about $5.

EXAMPLES: EZY Dose Tablet Cutter and Deluxe Pill Splitter.

■

REPORT #10

FREE HEALTH CARE MADE EASY

FREE HOSPITAL CARE...

If you don't have insurance coverage, even a very brief hospital stay can easily cost you tens of thousands of dollars and put you on the edge of bankruptcy.

Fortunately, now there is something you can do. If you need hospital care but cannot afford it and have no insurance or if you have already been in the hospital and cannot afford to pay the bill, try calling the Hill-Burton Hotline. Through this program, hundreds of participating hospitals and other health facilities provide free or low-cost medical care to patients who are unable to pay.

You could qualify for this assistance even if your income is double the poverty-level income guidelines and even if a medical bill has already been turned over to a collection agency.

FOR MORE INFORMATION: Hill-Burton Hotline. 800-638-0742, *www.hrsa.gov/hillburton/compliance-recovery.htm.*

FREE MEDICAL CARE...

How would you like to have the finest medical care money can buy...and not spend one penny for it? That is exactly what thousands of people are doing every year thanks to the National Institutes of Health (NIH) Clinical Center. The NIH is funded by the federal government and is one of the nation's leading medical research centers.

At any one time there may be more than 1,000 programs under way where researchers are studying the latest procedures in the treatment of every imaginable disease, including all types of cancer, heart disease and diabetes, to mention a few.

If your condition is one that is being studied, you might qualify for free medical care at the NIH hospital located in Bethesda, Maryland.

FOR MORE INFORMATION: National Institutes of Health, Patient Recruitment, Mark O. Hatfield Clinical Research Center, Bethesda, Maryland 20892. 800-411-1222, *www.cc.nih.gov*.

FREE EYE CARE...

The community service pages of your local newspaper occasionally will run announcements by organizations such as the Kiwanis or Lions Clubs. They offer free eyeglasses and eye examinations to elderly people who couldn't afford them otherwise.

Also, check with your state's Office of the Aging. There is a wide variety of eye-care programs offered, and many include free eye exams and free eyeglasses.

To locate your state's office along with other resources, call 800-677-1116 or go to *www.eldercare.gov*.

CONTACT LENSES FOR FREE...

If you wear contact lenses or are thinking of getting them, Johnson & Johnson would like you to try their Acuvue contacts for free. Go to *www.acuvue.com*, fill out the information requested and a free-trial pair certificate will be sent to you.

FREE OR ALMOST-FREE DENTAL CARE...

There are more than 50 dental schools in the United States, all operating clinics that provide basic services at great savings. That includes checkups, cleaning, X-rays and fillings.

More advanced services such as fitting bridges, dentures and implants may also be available. Student dentists do the work but are closely supervised by their professors.

BONUS: Care may even be free for conditions the professors are studying.

MORE INFORMATION: To locate a nearby dental school, log on to the American Dental Education Association's Web site at *www.adea.org.* Click on "Dental Schools & Allied Education Programs" and follow the links. Or call local universities and ask if they have dental schools.

Also, the dental society or association in each state has a list of dentists who volunteer their services to assist people who cannot afford proper dental care.

Source: **Matthew Lesko**, Kensington, MD–based best-selling author of more than 100 books on how to get free services and products, *www.lesko.com.*

■

BONUS REPORTS:

SMARTER HOME BUYING

Source: **Elizabeth Razzi,** author of *The Fearless Home Buyer* (Stewart, Tabori & Chang).

Making an offer on a house? Include the following contingencies, so you can be sure the home lives up to your expectations. *Insist on a home inspection* by a professional inspector to uncover defects. *Get extra inspections,* if warranted by the general inspector, by structural engineers or other professionals. *Make sure the house is insurable*—insurers are reluctant to write policies on homes in certain areas, such as those prone to wildfires and mud slides. Finally, *make your offer contingent* on finding a willing buyer for your current home—but you may need to agree to let the house's current owners continue marketing the home until you can make your offer firm.

■

SURPRISING WAYS TO BOOST YOUR CREDIT SCORE

Source: **Evan Hendricks,** editor of *Privacy Times,* and author of *Credit Scores & Credit Reports,* published by Privacy Times, Cabin John, MD.

The higher your credit score (which ranges from 300 to 850), the lower the interest rate you'll be charged on many loans, including mortgages. Being prudent with your spending doesn't necessarily help your credit score. **TO RAISE YOUR SCORE...**

• *Have several credit cards.* Otherwise, the lenders may have trouble deciding whether you are likely to pay multiple debts on time.

• *Watch your credit-use ratio.* A main factor in determining your score is the amount of your credit card balances versus credit limits. Keeping the balance below 30% of the limit on all of your cards will boost your score.

• *Don't consolidate debt onto a low-rate card and close the higher-rate account.* Doing so can raise your debt on the low-rate card above the 30% threshold. Instead, leave the high-rate card open. Pay off all your credit card balances, for example, with an installment loan, such as a bank personal loan, but leave the accounts open. The combination of decreasing your credit card balances and never being late on the installment will improve your credit score.

■

TRAVEL AND ENTERTAINMENT

2

TRAVEL AND ENTERTAINMENT

REPORT #11

HOW TO TRAVEL FOR NEXT TO NOTHING...OR FREE

Source: **Sue Goldstein,** creator of The Underground Shopper, a multimedia outlet that includes a Dallas-area call-in radio show on shopping and an Internet shopping site, *www.undergroundshopper.com.*

Two of the best ways to travel all over the world on an exceptionally tight budget...

COURIER FLIGHTS...

When a company needs to have an important document or package hand delivered, it might hire a courier to handle it. As a courier, you give up a portion of your check-on luggage allowance, which the company uses for its cargo. When you arrive, you deliver the package to the shipping agent's representative and your job is done.

Courier arrangements are most worthwhile for international flights. With nearly 40,000 courier flights every year, the destination choices are extensive. Flying from New York to Bangkok, for example, might cost you only $300 round-trip. A standard commercial flight to Bangkok typically costs more than $1,000. It's best to reserve at the last minute. The closer your desired departure date, the bigger your discount. There are times when a courier will be able to fly for free with just a few hours' notice.

Most courier companies expect you to stay for a specified period of time, usually anywhere from seven to 30 days. You are limited to one check-in piece of luggage and sometimes only one carry-on.

Tickets typically are nonrefundable and must be paid for in cash and picked up in person, often on the day of the flight. Most tickets are round-trip, and the return flights typically are open-ended. You can return anytime after your stint as a courier ends.

Courier flights depart from major cities, such as New York, Los Angeles, Chicago and Miami. Some courier firms charge a registration fee—$35 to $50—which gives you access to a wider range of ticket options and prices.

Where to book courier flights...

• *Air Courier Association/Cheap Trips.* $39.95 for annual membership plus a monthly fee of $4.99. 800-461-8556, *www.air courier.org.*

• *International Association of Air Travel Couriers.* $45 for annual domestic membership ($50 for international). 515-292-2458, *www.courier.org.*

FREE OR LOW-COST CRUISES...

If you are a gentleman between the ages of 45 and 75 and are well-groomed and well-spoken, cruise ships want you.

YOUR MISSION: To dance with and otherwise accompany the many unescorted women passengers. You might also help with dance classes and act as an escort on shore excursions as well as to dinner.

Gentlemen hosts need to be able to fox-trot, rumba, cha-cha and waltz. Cruise lines might ask you to audition at a dance studio in a nearby major city—they have relationships with studios around the country. In return, you get to see the world, meet people and enjoy gourmet feasts around the clock.

MOST IMPORTANT RULE: You must act professionally at all times. If you're caught sneaking extra dances or otherwise romancing particular passengers, you'll be asked to leave the ship at the next port and will have to get home on your own.

A gentlemen host is unpaid but receives a free cabin, discounts on drinks, laundry service and often free airfare. Booking agencies might charge a small fee—less than $30 per day. If you go directly to the cruise line, there's usually no fee.

To become a gentleman host...

• *Crystal Cruises.* 800-804-1500, *www.crystalcruises.com* (click on "Media Center," then "Fact Sheets," then "Ambassador Host Program for Singles").

• *Sixth Star Entertainment & Marketing.* 954-462-6760, *www. sixthstar.com.*

• *The Working Vacation.* 708-301-7535, *www.theworkingva cation.com.*

■

REPORT #12

LUXURY CRUISES FOR MUCH LESS

Source: **Joan Rattner Heilman,** an award-winning travel writer based in NY. She is author of *Unbelievably Good Deals and Great Adventures That You Absolutely Can't Get Unless You're Over 50* (McGraw-Hill).

The cruise ship business is now booming. Millions of Americans are taking vacations afloat every year, and six more huge passenger liners (including the largest cruise ship in the world, *Freedom of the Seas*) were launched in 2006.

There is such an overwhelming array of itineraries, ships, packages and prices today that it can seem almost impossible to know whether you're getting the right trip at the right price.

Here are more than a dozen smart strategies...

• *Get an early bird discount.* If you book from six months to a year before departure, most cruise lines will discount their published retail rates. You'll also get your first choice of cabin category and location. You must make a small deposit—perhaps $200 per person for a five-day cruise—but usually you may cancel without penalty up to 60 days before departure.

• *Look for off-season specials.* Schedule your trip when other people do not. For example, most people want to visit Alaska in the summer, so if you're looking for a more attractive rate, go in May or September. Cruise the Caribbean in the spring or summer, or try the Mediterranean in the winter. Avoid holidays and school vacation weeks. Of course, the trade-off may be the weather. For example, Athens can be downright chilly in the winter.

• *Take a "repositioning" cruise.* Some of the year's lowest rates can be found in the spring when ships relocate from their winter home ports in the Caribbean, Florida, Hawaii or Mexico to their summer bases in Europe, New York, Vancouver or Alaska.

The same goes for the late fall, when ships return to southern locations for the peak season that starts before Christmas.

"These can be the best bargains of the year," claims Jared Smith, president of icruise.com, one of the largest cruise brokers in the country. "They have unusual and unique itineraries, such as from the Caribbean through the Panama Canal, up the Pacific coast to Alaska, and are longer than the usual cruise, so they tend to appeal to people who really love to be at sea."

• *Find a last-minute deal.* Because the cruise lines want to keep their ships full, you can sometimes get good discounts by booking only a month or two before departure, when a line finds it still has unsold cabins. The downside is that you might not get a cruise you really want because the choice of ships and cabins will be limited. Search for ads in the newspaper, check the cruise line or on-line cruise brokers (see page 30).

• *Be flexible.* If you're willing to sail on a different date than you originally intended, sometimes even by only a week or two, you may be able to get the very same cabin on the same ship for significantly less money. And if you aren't rigid about your dates and itineraries, you'll have better luck nailing down a last-minute special.

• *Look for the two-for-one promotions.* On some sailings, two passengers can share a cabin for the price of one. These "twofers," however, are based on the full brochure rate, and in some cases, they do not include port charges and other fees that can be substantial. Airfare to and from the port city may also be extra. Another popular promotion is a "second passenger 50% off" deal, where one passenger pays a discounted rate and the second passenger pays only half of that.

• *Pick a port near home.* If you can find a cruise that departs from a port that's within driving distance of home, you won't have to spend money on airline tickets or hotels. According to Terry Dale, president of the CLIA (Cruise Line International Association), the trade organization of most of the major cruise lines, there are 32 home ports in North America today, and 75% of the US population lives within driving distance of one of them.

• *Snag a senior discount.* Cruise brokers frequently offer discounts to passengers over a certain age, usually 55, and their cabin mates of any age, especially on last-minute choices. The cruise lines, too, have similar promotions for sailings that are not expected to be full.

• *Go with a group.* Many lines will give you a reduced group rate. They may even toss in a free cabin if you organize a group that exceeds a specified minimum number of people, typically anywhere from six or eight to 16. Negotiate. You might even get upgrades or extra amenities.

• *Take the kids—or grandkids—for nothing.* Off-season sailings will frequently offer to take children free. Of course, that means you will all be in the same cabin—and with four to a cabin, it can get pretty crowded. But, remember, you probably won't be spending much time in your cabin.

• *Share the cabin.* If you're traveling with friends or relatives, you can save a bundle when they share your cabin by using the third and/or fourth berths. Sometimes third and fourth adults (not only children) may even go free. But if you are looking at an air/cruise package, make sure airfare is included for the *entire* group if you are not within driving distances of the port city.

• *Ask what's included.* Extra charges are not always included in the quoted price. Factor in all the port charges, taxes, handling fees and other costs before comparing deals.

• *Double check before you book.* Before booking a cruise, call the cruise line or broker or visit its Web site, because you may find a sale rate that's better than what you've decided upon. But make sure the cabin category and location and other important considerations are equivalent. Also try going to *www.cruisecom pete.com*, an on-line "auction" service that asks dozens of independent agents to give you quotes on prices for the ship, travel dates and cabin category you've chosen so you can compare the fares and have a greater chance of getting the best deal.

Here are some of the specialized cruise discount sites...

- *icruise.com,* 866-942-7847.
- *mustcruise.com,* 888-516-6306.
- *cruise411.com,* 800-553-7090.
- *1-800-cruises.com,* 800-278-4737.
- *7blueseas.com,* 800-242-1781.
- *cruise.com,* 888-333-3116.

You can also find discounts at *travelocity.com*, 877-815-5446, and *expedia.com*, 888-249-3978.

- **Consult a specialist.** After you've done your own research and have an idea of what you want, acquire the services of a travel agent or on-line retailer who specializes in cruises. An expert can help you sort everything out, find the best prices for your preferred itinerary, advise you on getting the best cabin and may even be able to throw in a few extras such as shipboard credit, shore excursions or a bottle of wine every night.

For a list of certified agents in your neighborhood, go to the Web site of CLIA at *www.cruising.org.* ■

REPORT #13

AMERICA'S 7 NATURAL WONDERS

Source: **Patricia Schultz,** New York City–based author of *1,000 Places to See Before You Die* and *1,000 Places to See in the United States Before You Die* (both from Workman, *www.workman.com/1000places*).

There are sights in America so breathtaking, destinations so inspiring, that those who see them remember the experiences for the rest of their lives. In a country as diverse and remarkable as the United States, the list of unforgettable places is almost endless. **BUT A FEW SPOTS TRULY STAND OUT...**

DENALI NATIONAL PARK, ALASKA...

Alaska is America's frontier, the state that best embodies our nation's sense of unconquered possibility, and Denali is Alaska's showplace. The six-million-plus-acre preserve features Mount McKinley, the tallest peak on the continent, plus remarkable wildlife—moose, caribou, elk and grizzly bear. Visit between late May and September, when the weather is best. The entry fee is $10 per individual...$20 per family...$5 per person for hikers (National Park Service, 907-683-2294, *www.nps.gov/dena*).

Camp Denali, a cluster of 17 rustic yet comfortable cabins in the park, is the best way to experience it. In addition to gourmet food, you'll have access to the camp's guides and naturalists, who lead backcountry tours and give talks. $425 per night per person, including meals, guided nature treks and other activities (907-683-2290, *www.campdenali.com*).

For a more affordable visit, stay at one of the hotels that is clustered around the park's entrance, such as the White Moose Lodge. $60 to $90* (800-481-1232, *www.whitemooselodge.com*). Go to *www.travelalaska.com* for more options.

Check with the National Park Service for camping information (see above).

CANYON DE CHELLY NATIONAL MONUMENT, ARIZONA...

The Grand Canyon is a stunning sight, but a memorable canyon experience of a different sort is the less crowded Canyon de Chelly (pronounced "shay") on Navajo Nation land in northeast Arizona, with a gateway entrance in Chinle. Unlike the Grand Canyon, it features clay and stone Native American dwellings that are more than 1,000 years old. Navajo guides help you explore and understand what you see. Free to enter the park, $15 per hour for a permit to hike or drive into the canyon accompanied by an authorized Navajo guide (928-674-5500, *www.nps.gov/cach*).

The simple, no-frills Thunderbird Lodge, with its all-Navajo staff, is the only hotel within the park. $60 to $155 (800-679-2473, *www.tbirdlodge.com*).

PACIFIC COAST HIGHWAY, CALIFORNIA...

The Pacific Coast Highway (Route 1) is the greatest drive in America. It winds though idyllic California towns, past grand mansions and along some of the most stunning coastline in the world. The most impressive stretch is from Santa Monica, just north of Los Angeles, up to Sonoma County, north of San Francisco. Worthwhile visits along the way include Hearst Castle in San Simeon. $24 (800-444-4445, *www.hearstcastle.org*)...

*All lodging prices are per room per night double-occupancy, unless otherwise noted.

picturesque Carmel (*www.carmelcalifornia.com*)…and the Big Sur region (*www.bigsurcalifornia.org*).

Big Sur is a particularly lovely place to spend the night. If money is no object, stay at the luxurious Ventana Inn & Spa for $485 and up (800-628-6500, *www.ventanainn.com*). Those with tighter budgets might consider Deetjen's Big Sur Inn, where a simple room with a shared bath can be had for as little as $75 (831-667-2377, *www.deetjens.com*).

MIDDLE FORK OF THE SALMON RIVER, IDAHO…

This waterway runs through the largest undeveloped region in the continental US, 20,000 square miles that look virtually the same as they did in the days of Lewis and Clark. Depending on the season, rafting down the Salmon River can offer anything from thrilling rapids to a leisurely journey. It's best to visit in May or June if you're looking for thrills…September for calm currents and relaxing fly-fishing…July or August for something in between.

Rocky Mountain River Tours has an impressive safety record and employs expert guides. Expect to spend $995 to $1,995 per person for a four- to six-day trip that includes specialty Dutch oven meals and camping gear. Book at least six months in advance (208-756-4808 [summer], 208-345-2400 *www.rocky mountainrivertours.com*).

GLACIER NATIONAL PARK, MONTANA…

This national park along the Canadian border is called Little Switzerland because of its glacier-carved terrain. There are hundreds of miles of hiking trails, or you can tour by car. Visit in summer to avoid snow. $25 for a seven-day vehicle permit (406-888-7800, *www.nps.gov/glac*).

Park-run lodging includes the rustic Many Glacier Hotel, with incredible views, for $125 and up…and Lake McDonald Lodge, which offers more modern comforts for $105 and up (406-892-2525, *www.glacierparkinc.com*).

GETTYSBURG NATIONAL MILITARY PARK AND CEMETERY, PENNSYLVANIA…

Walking around this Civil War battlefield where more than 50,000 men died is a moving experience. Monuments, gravestones and relics preserve the memory of the war. Visit between

July 1 and July 3 each year to witness battle reenactments by thousands of volunteers. Admission is free (717-334-1124, *www. nps.gov/gett*).

The Farnsworth House Inn bed-and-breakfast dates to 1810 and housed Confederate sharpshooters—you still can find bullet holes in the building. From $125 and up (717-334-8838, *www. farnsworthhouseinn.com*).

NORTHEAST KINGDOM, VERMONT...

Orleans, Essex and Caledonia counties in northeastern Vermont make up the Northeast Kingdom, marked by covered bridges, steepled churches and charming towns. In the fall, when the leaves change color, roads are packed with "leaf-peepers," so expect to move slowly (800-639-6379, *www.nekchamber.com*).

Among the great inns and B&Bs in the region is the Inn on the Common in Craftsbury Common, which dates to 1790. $185 and up during peak season (800-521-2233, *www.innon thecommon.com*).

∎

REPORT #14

DELUXE TRAVEL FOR LESS

Source: **Roy Prince,** owner of HomeExchange.com, featuring listings in more than 85 countries, Hermosa Beach, CA.

Looking for a less expensive vacation? Consider exchanging homes. This type of service is provided in California, New York, Paris, London and other locations.

ADVANTAGES: You eliminate hotel expenses and, often, car-rental fees—a car sometimes comes with the house—and save money on eating out.

TO FIND A HOME EXCHANGE: Post your own ad and answer ads for a fee on home-exchange Web sites, such as *www.home exchange.com...www.exchangehomes.com...www.digsville.com.*

BEFORE EXCHANGING: Build trust with your exchange partner with lots of pretrip communication...mention any concerns up front—if, for example, you don't permit any smoking in your home. All exchange partners should sign a written agreement and—for final assurance of commitment—exchange copies of their airline tickets. Exchangers who stay in your home for up to 30 days are considered guests and should be covered by your homeowner's insurance—verify this with your insurer. For any periods that are longer than 30 days, ask your insurance company about additional coverage.

■

REPORT #15

FREE GAS JUST FOR YOU

Independent hotels nationwide are providing special incentives to travelers who frequent them through the Frequent DriverMiles.com program.

Most participating hotels will reimburse you for a gasoline receipt dated the day you arrive (they buy your gas). Others provide discounts on room rates based on the number of miles you drive to get there.

Other incentives are available, as well as bargain rates to guests who book rooms through the program's Web site.

Member hotels are located in many US states, with more joining. Hotels are in all categories of quality and price range.

To find a hotel near your destination and get a good deal, visit *www.frequentdrivermiles.com*.

■

REPORT #16

WHAT YOUR CAR DEALER DOESN'T WANT YOU TO KNOW

Source: **Eric Peters**, automotive columnist in Washington, DC. He is author of *Automotive Atrocities!* (Motorbooks International). He owns a 1976 Pontiac Trans Am 455 and a 1964 Chevy Corvair Monza coupe.

Buying a used luxury car can be a smart way to get the ride you have always wanted without breaking the bank—as long as you know what to look for.

EXAMPLE: A 2006 Mercedes-Benz S-Class sedan currently sells for about $86,000. A four-year-old version of essentially the same vehicle has an average retail value of $50,000—a saving of about $36,000.

Today's luxury cars are extremely durable, so 50,000 miles on the odometer is no big deal. With gentle treatment and regular maintenance, a late-model luxury car can run well beyond 100,000 miles, largely free of trouble. In addition, many of the most desirable premium models have classic looks that change little over the years.

EXAMPLE: Jaguar XJ Series or Range Rover. A five- or even 10-year-old model still looks very much like a brand-new one.

WHAT TO WATCH OUT FOR...

Used luxury vehicles can be very expensive to maintain, particularly if they haven't been scrupulously serviced according to the manufacturer's recommendations.

EXAMPLE: Brake work on a high-end Mercedes-Benz can easily exceed $1,000.

IMPORTANT: Have any used vehicle thoroughly evaluated—all systems checked out—ideally by a technician at a new-car dealership for that particular make. Expect to spend between $100 and $200 for this evaluation.

Be wary of any used luxury car that doesn't have a complete record of service work—everything from oil and filter changes to other scheduled maintenance and repairs. If there are gaps in the record or it doesn't appear that a recommended or scheduled service was performed, ask for a price reduction equivalent to the cost of the service or pass on the deal.

WHERE TO LOOK...

Start by checking Edmunds.com, Autosite.com and the National Automobile Dealers Association's used-car value guides (*www.nada.com*) to get a sense of the retail/wholesale prices for any car that you're interested in.

Most major automakers have certified preowned (CPO) vehicle programs. CPO vehicles often are just off their original leases or were traded in with relatively low mileage. **SPECIFIC BENEFITS INCLUDE...**

• *Manufacturer-backed extended warranty coverage,* which is generally much more inclusive than dealer-backed coverage.

• *Service records*—usually available from the time that the vehicle was new.

• *Vehicle inspection and service prior to resale.* This cuts down on some expenses that often are involved in buying a used car, such as new brakes or tires.

Perhaps the best place to look for a properly maintained luxury car in good condition is in the classified ads of publications that cater to car club members devoted to the make/model you are interested in.

RECENT EXAMPLE: The BMW Car Club of America (864-250-0022, *www.bmwcca.org*) had several 2001 and 2002 models available for between $25,000 and $50,000.

To find other high-end car clubs, simply type the name of the car and the word "club" into a search engine, such as Google or Yahoo!. You'll be in touch with knowledgeable enthusiasts who can provide valuable advice.

OTHER RESOURCES: Publications that focus on specific makes can be found in major bookstores. *Hemmings Motor News* is a great general resource, available on-line (*www.hemmings.com*) and in print at major bookstores.

CLASSIEST USED CARS...

Some of my favorite used luxury cars...

• *1993 Cadillac Allante.* This beautiful convertible initially was plagued by an underpowered and problem-prone 4.1- and 4.5-liter V-8, but the engine was replaced in the final year of production by GM's superb 4.6-liter, 295-hp all-aluminum Northstar V-8. The '93s are the most desirable of the entire 1986–1993 production run. You can get a very nice Allante for less than $40,000.

• *Land Rover's legendary Range Rover 4.6 HSE.* It has been around in largely the same form for many years. The loaded 1999 model can go for less than $20,000. A new Range Rover costs about $74,000.

• *Lexus LS 400 and LS 430.* These exceptionally well-built, durable luxury sedans are some of the best used buys. A 2000 model can be found for between $21,000 and $26,000—a new LS sedan costs about $56,000.

• *1987-1991 Lincoln Mark VII LSC.* This is America's answer to the Mercedes-Benz SL. These large, sophisticated-looking coupes all feature powerful five-liter V-8s...high-capacity disc brakes…and air-ride suspension. Well-maintained examples are available for less than $15,000.

• *Mercedes E-Class Turbo Diesel* was one of the best midsize luxury sedans around. A 1999 E300 Turbo Diesel can be found for between $16,000 and $21,000. The base price of a new 2006 E-Class with a gas V-6 is about $51,000.

■

REPORT #17

HOW TO GET VIP SERVICE ALL THE TIME

Source: **Mark Brenner,** author of *Tipping for Success: Secrets for How to Get In and Get Great Service* (Brenmark House) and founder of Brenmark House, a marketing solutions think tank for companies that require branding, marketing, sales and advertising strategies, Sherman Oaks, CA, *www.brenmarkhouse.com.*

Anyone can get a last-minute reservation at a popular restaurant that is booked solid—*if* you know what to say and how to tip.

Here's what to do when you call at the last minute and are told no tables are available…

• *Ask to speak with the maitre d'.* Get his/her name before your call is transferred.

• *When the maitre d' picks up, address him by his first name, and give your own full name.* That creates the impression that you have been to the restaurant before and know him.

• *Give your name, and say with empathy, "I know how busy you are tonight.* But if you could find a way to have a table for me at 8 pm, I would be happy to take care of you the right way." This language may feel uncomfortable or cagey, but it is the language that service professionals recognize.

HELPFUL: Never mention a dollar figure—it is offensive and demeans his craft. Be specific in what you want. Otherwise you could end up eating at 5 pm or midnight.

• *If the answer is still no, take one last shot.* Say, "I don't mind waiting in the bar for a bit if it would help you out." Your flexibility lets him know that you are experienced and not unreasonable.

• *If you get a table, tip the maitre d' discreetly* (no one should ever see). Give him the folded bill(s) in your handshake.

The tip amount depends on the caliber of the restaurant, how badly you want to get in and how hard the maitre d' had to work to get you the table—$10 is enough for a good restaurant on a typical night...$20 to $50 for more extreme circumstances, such as conventions, holidays, etc.

VALET PARKING: KEEPING YOUR CAR UP FRONT...

When your waiter hands over your check, hand him/her your valet ticket stub, and ask him to give it to the valet, so that your car is waiting up front by the time you pay the bill and leave the restaurant.

■

REPORT #18

PLAY THE SLOTS AND WIN

Source: **Victor H. Royer,** gambling industry consultant in Las Vegas who has worked for some of the leading casinos and slot machine manufacturers. He is author of many books on casino gambling, including *Powerful Profits from Slots* (Kensington).

Until the mid-1980s, slot machines truly were one-armed bandits. The house usually had an advantage of 20%—and sometimes even more.

Since then, casinos have come to rely on slots players for most of their revenues. This has created competition among casinos and dramatically sweetened the odds for players.

Here's how to maximize your chances of winning...

WHERE TO PLAY...

• *Visit Vegas.* Slot machines in Las Vegas offer the best odds in the country, giving the house an advantage of just 2% to 4%. Only an expert blackjack player has better odds in a casino. But beware—slot machines in bars or other noncasino locations generally offer terrible odds.

Slots in Reno and in the tribal casinos of the East Coast are not quite as advantageous as those in Las Vegas, but they're still better than those in Atlantic City, where house advantages of 6% to 8% are common. Riverboat and tribal casinos of the Midwest generally provide the worst odds, with house advantages of as much as 10%.

• *Look for high-profile "slot islands."* Casinos want gamblers to see people winning. In most casinos, slot islands—clusters of four to six slot machines (sometimes on slightly raised platforms)—are placed where aisles intersect. These machines often offer the best chance of a jackpot.

Also try slot machines located near the main casino cage, where winnings are collected.

• *Avoid slot machines near table games.* Casinos don't want the noise of slot machine payouts to disturb people playing blackjack or craps.

Also skip slot machines located near buffet lines. Casinos know that people standing in line will play the slots out of boredom even without frequent payoffs.

PICK THE RIGHT MACHINE...

• *Choose $1 slots.* Quarter slot machines usually have much lower payback rates than $1 machines. The $5 or $10 slots offer even better odds, but most recreational gamblers would go through their money much too fast to make these machines worthwhile and enjoyable.

• *Choose three-reel machines.* These slots tend to have slightly better odds.

• *Look for "double-up" or "triple-up" machines.* These provide two or three times the usual payout in addition to marginally better odds.

MY FAVORITES: All reel and video slots from IGT, including Double Diamond, Triple Diamond, Triple Lucky 7s and Triple Double Dollars.

• *Don't invest too much in "progressive" slots.* These machines —which offer a shot at huge jackpots that build up over time, sometimes into the millions of dollars—typically have poor odds. They exist for the same reason that lotteries exist—people like to dream big.

MORE STRATEGIES...

• *Bet the most coins per pull that a machine allows.* The majority of slot machines provide a better percentage return when more coins are played.

EXAMPLE: The top jackpot on a $1 machine might be $800 if a single $1 coin is played.

However, if two $1 coins are played simultaneously, the jackpot becomes $2,000—that is a 150% increase in return for a 100% increase in your investment.

• *Play after the crowds.* Most slot machine players visit the casinos between the hours of 5 pm and 11 pm. If you play just after all the crowds leave, the slot machines are likely to be full of their money. That's when you will have a better chance of finding a machine that will produce a winning jackpot.

• *Switch machines if you get a few "almost" jackpots.* If a machine comes close to a jackpot several times—say, all three sevens are visible but not in the payout line—that doesn't mean it is about to pay off. My experience suggests it is less likely to hit the jackpot anytime soon.

■

REPORT #19

UNTOLD SECRETS TO WINNING AT TEXAS HOLD 'EM

Source: **Phil Hellmuth, Jr.,** nine-time World Series of Poker champion and one of the most respected Texas Hold 'Em tournament players. He is author of *Phil Hellmuth's Texas Hold 'Em* (HarperTorch) and *Play Poker Like the Pros* (Harper-Collins). His Web site is *www.philhellmuth.com.*

Texas Hold 'Em, the poker game favored by professional poker players, is rapidly becoming the favorite game of amateurs as well.

The rules of Texas Hold 'Em are simple. Each player receives two cards facedown. After one round of betting, three cards are dealt face up for players to share (called the "flop"). Then there's a second round of betting, a fourth card up (the "turn"), a third round of betting, a final up card (the "river"), and one more round of betting.

Players make their best five-card hands out of their two "pocket" cards and the five "community cards" face up on the table. While the rules are easy to learn, those who know Texas Hold 'Em only from watching TV tournaments often run into trouble when they try to play. **HERE, WINNING STRATEGIES…**

• *Start tight.* When you watch poker on TV, the professionals seem to play lots of hands. That's because TV coverage shows only key hands. In most home games, the bets are small, so the best strategy is to play extremely "tight," folding most of the hands you're dealt. Play only when dealt one of the 10 best two-card starting hands—pairs of 7s or higher, or an ace-king or ace-queen. When you do get one of these great starting hands, always raise or reraise—don't just call (match a bet).

EXCEPTION: If a very conservative player already has made a big bet in front of you and you have a pair of 7s, 8s or 9s, you should fold.

Playing only strong hands will boost your odds of survival while you learn and perfect your game, and you will earn a reputation for playing only great cards, which will make bluffing easier later on.

• *Raise after the flop even if it didn't help you.* The flop is the first three community cards turned over. Often, they won't be the cards you want—but your opponents may not want them either. Rather than not betting on a disappointing flop, make a bet to find out where you're at. Maybe your opponents will fold or call rather than raise, indicating that you might not be in such bad shape after all. (If a raise and a reraise are made before it's your turn to bet, fold if your hand isn't strong.)

EXAMPLE: You hold 10-10, and the flop comes king-queen-2. With two cards on the table higher than your 10s, someone might have hit a higher pair, putting you at a big disadvantage—or then again, maybe no one was holding a king or a queen. If you don't bet, someone else likely will—and you'll have to assume he/she made his hand and fold. If you do make a small bet and no one raises, it may tell you that you're still ahead and may confuse your opponents.

• *Learn to read your opponents.* Even after you fold, time at the poker table shouldn't be wasted. Pick one or two of your opponents and try to guess what cards they're holding based on their behavior and bets. Watch for patterns. Do they only raise on big hands? Do they act especially confident when they have nothing?

• *"Slow play" the occasional big hand.* Once your opponents get used to you betting big on the great hands, throw them a curve. If you have ace-ace or king-king, call before the flop. You might make the other players believe that your hand is weak and win a bigger pot. Even if you don't, you'll make it harder for them to figure out what you have later.

In no-limit or pot-limit Hold 'Em, in which pots can grow large, it might be worth seeing a flop (matching a bet before the flop) with a small pair if you can do so cheaply. The odds of hitting three of a kind still are against you, but if you do hit you might be able to build a big enough pot to make it worthwhile.

■

REPORT #20

THE GARDEN-PEST PROBLEM-SOLVER

> *Source:* **Christine Bucks,** garden book editor at Rodale Inc., publisher of books and magazines, Emmaus, PA. She has edited more than 20 gardening books, including *Great Garden Fix-Its: Organic Remedies for Everything from Aphids to Weeds* (Rodale), a compendium of garden solutions from dozens of successful gardeners.

When spring is here, it's not long before critters invade your garden. Whether it's beetles feasting on your flowers or deer devouring the tomato plants, there are several ways to get rid of garden pests without resorting to the use of dangerous poisons to get rid of them. **HERE'S HOW...**

BUGS...

• *Aphids.* These tiny, green-gray bugs can suck the life from vegetables, flowers and tree leaves. They usually travel in large swarms so, despite their small size, they can quickly devastate a garden.

Aphids are repelled by the scent of citrus rind. Combine one tablespoon of freshly grated citrus rind with one pint of boiling water, steep overnight, strain the mixture through a coffee filter, then pour it into a spray bottle. Add three drops of dishwashing liquid, and spray affected plants and those nearby.

If that doesn't do it, buy an insecticidal soap at a garden store. Test it on one or two plants—insecticidal soaps may do as much damage as aphids. If the sprayed plants show signs of leaf browning, curling or spotting within the next three days, don't use the soap. Otherwise, spray aphid-affected plants every five to seven days as long as the problem persists. Be sure to spray the undersides of leaves as well as the tops.

• *Japanese beetles.* These shiny, half-inch-long copper-colored beetles with green and white markings are a familiar but unwelcome sight to gardeners in the eastern US. Japanese beetles are particularly fond of rosebushes and of grape and raspberry plants, but they'll eat virtually any plant.

To fight back, put soapy water in a wide bowl and hold it under the branches of beetle-affected plants. Gently shake the branches. Most of the beetles will drop into the bowl and drown.

A long-term solution is to apply milky spore disease powder —available at garden stores—to your lawn near your garden as directed on the label. In two to five years, the disease will take hold, killing beetle grubs in the soil. The disease is harmless to humans, pets and beneficial insects.

• *Slugs and snails.* These pests eat holes through broad-leaf plants. To limit damage, place a few empty tuna or cat food cans in the soil up to their brims. Then pour beer into them. Slugs and snails are attracted to beer and drown in the cans. Use long-handled tweezers to remove the dead pests, or dump the contents—beer and all—on your compost pile. Then add more beer to the cans. Install beer traps in the spring before slugs and snails have a chance to reproduce.

Also put a few boards on the ground in your garden. Slugs and snails love the moist shade underneath. Every day or two, pick up the boards and scrape the collected critters into a pail of soapy water. Remove the boards in autumn so that slugs and snails can't seek shelter there during cold weather.

HELPFUL: You will substantially reduce your garden's slug and snail population if you water your garden in the morning rather than the afternoon. That way, the soil will be dry by night, when these creatures are active, robbing them of the moisture that they need to survive.

ANIMALS...

• *Deer.* Deer are naturally mistrustful of certain scents. You can hang cheesecloth bags of human hair (hair is available at salons and barber shops) around your garden. Dirty socks or bags of soap may also do the trick.

Organic deer-repellent sprays, such as Deer Away Big Game Repellent and Hinder Deer, have odors that are offensive to deer but not to humans. You can expect to spend $25 and up per gallon at a garden store. Odor-based solutions such as these will not stop all deer, but they can cut plant loss in your garden by 30% to 50%.

The only way to stop most deer is with an electric fence. Expect to spend several hundred dollars at a home or garden store for a fence kit large enough to protect a 50-by-50-foot garden. To keep deer from jumping over your fence, smear peanut butter on aluminum foil tabs and attach them to the fence (always turn off the power before touching the fence). Deer that lick the peanut butter will receive a small shock and learn that your garden is best avoided. An electric fence is not an option for households with young children.

You also can switch to plants that deer don't like—or create a living fence of these plants around your yard.

FLOWERS: Begonias, daffodils, foxglove, globe thistle, iris, lavender, marigolds, meadow saffron, peony, scented geraniums, snapdragons, stars of Persia, sweet alyssum, strawflowers, yarrow, zinnias.

TREES AND BUSHES: American holly, boxwoods, Caucasian daphne, Sawara false cypress, Japanese pieris, northern red oak, pine, red osier dogwood, rugosa rose, spruce.

• *Rabbits.* Rabbits can decimate gardens, consuming everything from vegetables to seedlings. If rabbits are the culprits, you'll find hard, pea-sized dark brown droppings in neat piles.

You can try scaring rabbits away with fake snakes. Cut an old garden hose into serpentlike lengths, and place the pieces throughout your garden.

If that doesn't work, another way to protect your garden is to construct a two- to three-foot-high chicken wire fence around it. The fence must extend at least six inches beneath the ground so rabbits can't burrow under it.

• *Voles.* These tiny rodents can consume close to their body weight in tubers and bulbs each day as they tunnel through your garden.

When you plant bulbs, arrange a handful of sharp crushed gravel around them in the holes to keep voles away. Remove wood chips and mulch from the vicinity of young trees and shrubs in autumn so that voles have less cover during cold weather, when they eat mainly tree roots.

Gardeners with serious vole problems can plant their crops in wooden frames with quarter-inch or smaller wire mesh stapled to the bottom (frames are available at garden stores). The mesh allows roots to grow out but prevents voles from tunneling in. Or grow daffodils, one of the few garden bulbs that voles (and squirrels) won't eat.

■

RETIREMENT

RETIREMENT

REPORT #21

RETIRE EARLIER AND RICHER THAN YOU THOUGHT

Source: **Robert J. Reby, CFP**, president, Robert J. Reby & Co., a firm which advises clients on how to preserve and increase their wealth, Danbury, CT.

Retiring before you reach age 65 may be tempting—but it also can be risky.

The primary reason is inflation. Even a modest increase in prices has a huge cumulative effect over time, and Americans today are living longer than ever. The federal government calculates that a 50-year-old American woman will live to an average age of 80...a man, to about 75.

If prices rise by just 2% a year, your expenses will increase by nearly 50% in 20 years. At 4% inflation, they actually will more than double.

A good way to determine your yearly lifestyle needs is to add up six months of your fixed expenses—including mortgage payments, income taxes, property taxes and insurance. Also look back six months in your checkbook and credit card statements for any expenses that may have been left out. Double the amount you spent during those six months to arrive at your yearly income need.

Here are case histories of some of my clients who wanted to retire early and were able to pull it off...

TOM AND JULIA...

Five years ago, Tom, then 58, worked as an auto mechanic. His wife, Julia, 57, worked at a department store. Together, they earned about $125,000 a year. Since both were unhappy with their jobs, they wanted to retire early. Neither had a pension, but they were conscientious savers and hoped that their $470,000 investment portfolio would generate enough income for them to live on.

INCOME NEED: $40,000 a year, including $7,500 for property and income taxes...$8,000 for two health insurance policies... and $24,500 (about $2,000 a month) for all other expenditures—food, home maintenance and repairs, entertainment, travel, utilities, car and homeowners insurance, etc.

DECISION: I advised Tom and Julia against retiring early, but I urged them both to find more satisfying work. Their investment portfolio would have to grow by 8.5% a year in order to generate the necessary annual income of $40,000. A more realistic return assumption would be between 7% and 8% per year.

Retirees should never take so much out of their portfolios that they can't continue to grow *and* outpace inflation. Today, most retirees should invest in stocks and bonds that together earn an average of about 7% and should withdraw no more than 5% a year. The two-percentage-point differential will offset inflation.

What if inflation were to exceed 2%? They would have to live on a smaller percentage of their assets or find additional sources of income. They rejected my suggestion that they consider selling their home and buy a less expensive one, but a high inflation rate could force them to rethink that decision.

I advised Tom and Julia to continue working for five years. During that time, their portfolio would grow at about $35,000 a year. They could save another $25,000 a year from their salaries. In five years, their portfolio would reach approximately $770,000. At that point, they could consider retiring.

TODAY: At ages 63 and 62, respectively, Tom and Julia are retired and close to accessing their Social Security benefits, which would allow them to take less income from their savings. Perhaps they will be able to withdraw 4% to 5% from their portfolio instead of the 6% that they withdraw now.

LESSON: Don't overestimate your savings. Your nest egg of nearly $500,000 may sound impressive, but it won't go far if you stop working too soon or if you need considerable income from it.

RON AND CAROL...

Three years ago, Ron, then 54, made about $80,000 a year as a telecommunications engineer. His wife, Carol, then 53, sold real estate and earned $30,000 to $50,000 per year, depending on her commissions.

Ron lost his job when his company downsized. Both Ron and Carol wanted to retire, but they were willing to consider having one of them continue working. Of course, for Ron to continue to work, he would have to find another job.

INCOME NEED: The couple calculated that they would need $40,000 a year for their retirement. Their income-producing assets included Carol's IRA, which was worth about $200,000.

Ron and Carol decided against long-term-care insurance, which would have cost about $5,000 per year for both. Like many other couples, they're taking a chance that their assets will grow enough to cover the cost of long-term care if it is needed. (I advised partial insurance, but they did not follow that advice.)

Ron's pension fund could not be tapped for monthly income payments before age 65. Until then, the assets were available to him only in a lump-sum payout of $260,000.

DECISION: I advised Carol to keep working and Ron to withdraw the $260,000 pension in a lump sum. He rolled it over to an IRA and began taking distributions.

There's normally a 10% tax penalty on early withdrawals from IRAs, but Ron took advantage of Code Section 72(t), which allows IRA holders to avoid the penalty as long as withdrawals last for five years or until the age of 59½, whichever occurs later. Under a complex IRS formula, Ron was required to withdraw

$23,000 per year, or 5% of their total nest egg of $460,000 ($200,000 + $260,000). Meanwhile, Ron and Carol's combined retirement assets could be expected to grow at about 7%.

Since the $23,000 a year in income was short of the $40,000 that they needed, Carol would have to continue working full-time to add to their capital.

TODAY: Their assets stand at about $600,000—the result of growth in the couple's $460,000 nest egg and additional annual investments by Carol. They hope to build their nest egg up to $1 million by 2013, when they will be 65 and 64, respectively. Then Carol can retire and they can conservatively take $45,000 a year (4.5% a year) to supplement Social Security.

LESSON: Don't view retiring early as an all-or-nothing proposition. Continuing to work part-time—or having one spouse continue working full-time—often is a better option.

BOB AND MARIA...

Bob and Maria, both 55, recently faced a decision that many must make these days. His employer, a computer company, offered him an early retirement package with a choice of starting pension benefits immediately or, to get a higher monthly benefit, waiting until he was 62. (She didn't earn any income.)

The couple had to decide whether the early pension benefit—plus income from $550,000 worth of other assets—would be enough to maintain their lifestyle. Bob also needed $10,000 of seed capital to start his own part-time consulting business.

INCOME NEED: They estimated their total monthly expenses at $6,000, or $72,000 a year.

The early pension benefit came to approximately $4,000 a month, versus $4,800 at age 62. There was no provision in the pension plan for a lump-sum payout.

DECISION: Despite the prospect of a higher pension benefit at age 62, I advised Bob to begin drawing benefits immediately, at age 55. Doing so would enable him and Maria to retire early and Bob to launch his second career part-time.

The additional $2,000 a month needed to maintain their lifestyle would come from their $550,000 investment portfolio, at a withdrawal rate of approximately 4.5% per year.

REASON: If Bob waited until age 62 to start taking his pension benefits, he would receive only $800 more a month, but over the intervening seven years, he would forgo $336,000—based on $4,000 a month. Moreover, the couple's $550,000 in other assets wouldn't produce enough to live on, allow Bob to start his consulting business and cover inflation.

Another factor in Maria and Bob's decision—whether his pension's survivorship benefit would be adequate to support Maria if she were to outlive him. She would receive $2,400 a month, assuming Bob waited until age 62 to take benefits. (Payments would be $2,000 if he started to take benefits before age 62.)

Since the pension would not provide adequately for her, I suggested that Bob purchase life insurance. A male nonsmoker pays about $500 a month for a $500,000 policy at age 55. Bob would have to withdraw this money from his portfolio. Fortunately, he had the resources to do this.

Purchasing insurance also can be a worthwhile strategy for couples who don't have pensions. For easy comparison shopping, you can find free life insurance quotes at *www.insure. com* or *www.accuquote.com*.

LESSON: It's not always best to put off taking pension or Social Security benefits to get a higher payout in the future. Make sure you do the math before you decide.

■

REPORT #22

FUN RETIREMENT JOBS THAT PAY A LOT OF MONEY

Source: **Joanne Fritz, PhD,** a "not yet retired" entrepreneur in her mid-60s based in Oro Valley, AZ, formerly worked in higher education. Her Web site, *www. second50years.com,* provides information, services and products to people age 50 and older who want to continue to be productive in retirement.

Retirement is an opportunity to do what you love and are good at. And if you want to earn money, you can turn your passion and experience into a new source of income.

Review your interests—horseback riding, golf, animals, crafts, books, garage sales, etc. Chances are you can find extra income in those areas.

Perhaps you have built up a lifetime of expertise in a particular field—accounting, organizing events, writing, investing, counseling, teaching. Can you translate this into a paying retirement position? Or create a business from your interests or expertise? **HERE ARE SOME EXAMPLES...**

• *Barbara,* retired for 10 years, took an Elderhostel trip and enjoyed it so much that she used her previous experience in the corporate world to get a job as program coordinator with two of the universities that run Elderhostel. She runs half a dozen five- to 10-day programs per year, receiving up to $750 per program, and gets to see historical sites, museums and symphonies. To investigate this line of work, go to Elderhostel (*www.elderhostel.org*).

• *Tom and Jean* responded to an ad for house sitters and now look after haciendas in Mexico. This paid work gives them time and money to pursue their hobbies and interests.

• *Nadine* worked as an interior designer for many years. In retirement, she buys and sells small, older homes in her city's historical area to fix up and resell.

• *Don,* an outdoorsman, also retired, now works every summer at the concession at the North Rim of the Grand Canyon.

For jobs in great locations, such as a reservation clerk in a posh hotel or at a gift shop in a scenic park, visit *www.cool works.com*. (There's a specific page for older workers—click on "Older and Bolder.")

START YOUR OWN BUSINESS...

You don't have to reenter corporate America. Instead, you can carve out your own niche in the business world by starting your own company. **SOME EXAMPLES...**

• *Bill* used his previous experience in sales to start his own small company as a distributor for *Entrepreneur Magazine's* "start-up" manuals. He also became a business broker to help people buy and sell businesses. He runs all his activities from home and has plenty of time for travel with his wife.

• *Mary,* retired from a corporate job, had been a biology teacher early in her career. Before retiring, she took classes at a botanical garden to become certified as a "master gardener." She now grows plants to sell and provides landscape design for home owners.

• *Sheldon* didn't want to retire as chief executive of two companies but was forced to. He then bought a hotel so he could continue to run a business—and live the high life to boot.

• *Sue* started her own cleaning company, hiring teams of workers (some of whom are retirees) to do the cleaning.

• *Cynthia and Matt,* full-time RVers, supplement their retirement income selling odds and ends on eBay. They go to garage sales, auctions and estate sales to find bargains that they can resell through on-line auctions.

MORE EXAMPLES...

Looking for ideas on what to do? Let your imagination take off. HERE ARE MORE IDEAS TO CONSIDER...

• *Book lovers can sell their used editions on-line* through eBay (*www.eBay.com*) and Amazon (*www.amazon.com*). There's no need for an advertising budget. Hunt for merchandise to sell at garage sales, flea markets, library sales and thrift shops (*http://bookologist.com*).

• *Craftspeople can participate in craft fairs at local community centers and city and county fairs.* Build a customer list (collect names and phone numbers and e-mail addresses) so you can continue to sell directly to interested buyers.

• *Information addicts can create tips booklets to sell on-line.* Use your knowledge to teach others something of value about a hobby or a skill.

• *Travel aficionados can become home-based travel agents, full or part time.* To set up an account with a supplier (such as a cruise line or an airline), you need an agency account number from the International Association of Travel Agents Network (IATAN, *www.iatan.org*), Cruise Lines International Association (CLIA, *www.cruising.org*) or Airlines Reporting Corporation (ARC, *www.arccorp.com*).

Team up with a travel agency to become an independent agent to see if this business is for you (you can get your own license down the road).

CAUTION: Check your state's law on licensing and registration requirements for travel agents.

ON-LINE HELP...

If you still don't have an inkling of what you want to do or how to go about finding out, there's plenty of on-line help available. **SOME USEFUL SITES TO INVESTIGATE...**

• *AARP* (*www.aarp.org*) for information and numerous resources on working.

• *2 Young 2 Retire* (*www.2young2retire.com*) for ideas and examples of people changing the face of retirement.

• *Seniors4Hire* (*www.seniors4hire.org*) featuring free registration for people age 50 and older looking for jobs.

• *Senior Job Bank* (*www.seniorjobbank.com*), a referral service listing part-time flexible and temporary jobs.

• *Retired Worker U.S.* (*www.theretiredworker.com*) allows you to create an on-line profile (no résumés are used), which may attract employers.

■

REPORT #23

HOW TO WRITE YOUR LIFE STORY!

Source: **Joan R. Neubauer,** author of several books, including *From Memories to Manuscript: The Five-Step Method of Writing Your Life Story* (Ancestry) and *The Complete Idiot's Guide to Journaling* (Alpha). Based in Georgetown, TX, she teaches classes and conducts workshops on a variety of topics, from writing to business.

Everyone has unique life experiences that he/she should preserve for future generations. Writing your autobiography is the perfect way to tell your story and pass on lessons.

1. RESEARCH...

Before you start to write a single word, be sure to have all of your facts in hand...

• *Remember.* Buy yourself a stack of index cards and begin remembering the times of your life. Record a single event on each index card in a single sentence or phrase. Add the date if you can remember that.

Do this for all the events you think you would like to include in the book. You hold the key to how many index cards you end up with because it's up to you how much detail you will include in your book. Ask yourself questions that will help jog your memory—who, what, where, when, why and how.

EXAMPLES: Where was I born? Where did I live growing up?

Keep a binder, index cards or a tape recorder handy at all times to document recollections. Cards are easy to tote along to the library or wherever you're taking notes.

Smells will often evoke recollections for your autobiography. For instance, lilacs may help you remember more about a particular time in your childhood.

• *Gather information.* Talk with friends and relatives about times past, look through old photo albums, review old record books in your church library or town hall and go to the library to access facts and figures.

Some communities have societies dedicated to local history and genealogy. Check out your *Yellow Pages* or local library to find one in your area. The Church of Jesus Christ of Latter-day Saints (Mormon) also has genealogical resources available to the public at their local Family History Centers. Check their Web site at *www.familysearch.org.*

2. ORGANIZE...

After you've gathered your information, organize it...

• *Create a time line.* Organize all your material by milestones—graduations, weddings, births, job changes.

On a sheet of paper, draw a horizontal line. Starting from the left, fill in when you were born and then, moving to the right, fill in when you started school, etc.

• *Arrange the facts.* Create an outline for your story by using one (or a combination) of two ways to organize...

• Chronological—proceed in sequence. Each chapter of your life can be grouped in 10-year periods.

• By subject—group reminiscences into categories, such as education, romance, raising children, career, travel, etc. Each topic can then be handled chronologically.

Keep the reader in mind. Make sure the events flow logically from one to the other.

3. WRITE...

Use a computer, if you can, to set your story down. It will check your spelling and grammar. It also has features that allow you to easily refine your draft.

Keep the autobiography interesting by asking yourself key questions as you write...

• *Does this incident tell the reader something important about my life?*

• *Will this episode move the book along or bog it down?*

• *Must I include every person I ever met or every event in my life?*

To bring the scenes to life, write in the first person so that the story has your voice. Set the mood by using one or more of the five senses in each scene you describe.

EXAMPLE: We sat on the porch on those summer nights. The streetlights cast dancing shadows across the sidewalk as people strolled by and cars quietly passed. Gentle breezes carried the scent of honeysuckle from the field across the street.

My cousin and I flipped baseball cards against the brick wall of the house. "OK, so you won my cards," my cousin said, "I'll trade you my Willie Mays if you give them back." I was tempted, but didn't have the heart to take his Willie Mays, so I handed his cards back to him.

"Here. You owe me a pretzel at school tomorrow."

Particulars make the difference between competent writing and wonderful writing. It always helps to use dialogue wherever possible.

4. EDIT...

After you have finished writing, put the project aside for a while. You need to be detached and objective about the story when editing it.

You may need to edit your manuscript several times before it reads well. You're bound to see things that need to be changed with each pass.

Change verbs that end in "ing" to simple past tense (verbs that end in "d" or "ed").

Use the past tense to make your writing active (more definite and stronger).

EXAMPLES: Instead of "I was going," use "I went." Instead of "I could see," use "I saw."

Use grammar and style reference books—a good dictionary usually will provide all the guidance you require in terms of spelling and punctuation. *Merriam-Webster's Collegiate Dictionary* includes "A Handbook of Style" among its sections. And all writers can benefit from *Roget's International Thesaurus*.

5. PUBLISH...

Once you have written your story, consider publishing your book using print-on-demand (POD) technology, available from POD self-publishing companies.

WordWright.biz (*www.wordwright.biz*, 877-380-3321), specializes in helping new authors write, publish and distribute their stories. Their memoirs take a variety of forms, from poetry to prose. They can publish as few as 25 copies for family and friends.

■

REPORT #24

ERASE WRINKLES INSTANTLY

Source: **Barry DiBernardo, MD,** board-certified plastic surgeon and spokesperson for the American Society for Aesthetic Plastic Surgery, where he is on the nonsurgical procedures committee. The director of New Jersey Plastic Surgery, a private practice in Montclair, NJ, he is also chief of plastic surgery at Mountainside Hospital, also in Montclair.

In recent years, the science of reducing wrinkles has been transformed by the introduction of remarkable new devices and treatments that don't involve surgery. There are several developments that could help both men and women to look and feel better if they are concerned about wrinkles. HERE ARE THE LATEST INNOVATIONS...

• *Digital imaging machine that provides a computerized analysis of your skin.* A device called *Visia*, made by Canfield Clinical Systems, uses a computer-aided digital camera to analyze the facial skin in minute detail. It gives doctors an unprecedented ability to diagnose skin conditions and monitor the effectiveness of various treatments. On the market since 2002, Visia is now becoming widely available.

HOW IT WORKS: With the patient's head immobilized, digital photographs are taken under different types of light to identify the specific location and depth of various skin features, including wrinkles, brown spots, enlarged pores and acne. An ultraviolet light is used to scan for latent sun damage, which will emerge as the patient gets older.

When the analysis is complete, the patient's profile is matched against a database containing thousands of profiles. A percentile score shows how the patient's skin compares with that of people of similar age, gender and skin type. This analysis can then be used to guide doctors in prescribing and administering treatments. On subsequent visits, new digital images are taken to measure how well the skin is responding.

• *Laser treatment that stimulates skin to renew itself. Intense pulsed light (IPL) photorejuvenation* is becoming the treatment of choice for eliminating fine wrinkles, brown spots, broken capillaries and birthmarks—all without any recovery time.

HOW IT WORKS: This treatment produces light pulses at a variety of wavelengths, which penetrate the skin to different depths, depending on the problem being treated (brown spots tend to lie near the surface, for example, while broken capillaries are slightly below). This allows blemishes to be treated precisely without damaging surrounding tissue. Even better, IPL can penetrate below the top layer of skin (epidermis) to stimulate the cells that produce collagen and elastin—naturally occurring tissues that make skin more firm and elastic, and which we tend to lose as we get older. IPL photorejuvenation reverses this aging effect, making skin tighter and plumper.

While IPL has been around for a number of years, a new machine called the *Lumenis One* (manufactured by Lumenis) represents a significant advance over previous IPL devices. Among other things, its computer has an improved ability to deliver light at exactly the right location. This new device is so good at removing difficult-to-treat blemishes—and rejuvenating the skin—that even longtime patients praise its effectiveness. This treatment is available in most states. To find a practitioner in your area, call Lumenis at 877-586-3647.

Sessions last about 20 minutes. Typically, patients undergo a series of IPL treatments over several weeks, followed up by a maintenance treatment every six months. With older IPL technology, treatments lasted for 45 minutes, but the maintenance intervals were the same as for the new technology.

COST: $200 to $500 per treatment.

• *Radio frequency devices* that use radio frequency to tighten up the skin have been available for about four years, but a new device called *Titan* (manufactured by Cutera) represents a huge improvement over previous machines—it is safer, more effective and less expensive. It is available throughout the US and abroad. Radio frequency devices operate in the infrared range to heat the tissue under the skin surface, causing loose skin and its underlying collagen to contract and tighten. The treatment is effective even on large wrinkles. Since it doesn't remove any layers of skin, there is no flaking or redness following the treatment, eliminating the need for recovery time.

Radio frequency treatment is currently FDA approved for use on the forehead and around the eyes. Approval is pending for use on cheek folds and the neck area. A series of treatments may be needed for optimal results. It is not yet known how long results last.

COST: $250 to $2,000 a treatment, depending on the area covered and amount of time involved.

• *Hyaluronic filler that replaces collagen.* Deeper lines can be temporarily eliminated by injecting a filler material into the fat layer directly beneath the depressed area. Until recently, the only filler approved for use in the US was bovine collagen, derived from cattle. Collagen injections will last about three months and require allergy testing before use.

In December 2003, the FDA approved Restylane, a hyaluronic acid product already available in some 60 countries. Since hyaluronic acid occurs naturally in humans (it's the material between your cells), it's nonallergenic, and no skin test is needed. Restylane injections also last much longer than collagen injections—typically up to a year. Many dermatologists and aesthetic surgeons now use Restylane exclusively, while others continue to offer both Restylane and collagen.

COST: $500 to $1,500 per treatment.

MULTI-TREATMENT SKIN MAINTENANCE...

Taking advantage of the array of new tools described above, many people are now adopting a maintenance program where they see a doctor (either a plastic surgeon, dermatologist or other medical doctor who has been trained to perform aesthetic services) every six months for IPL treatment and Botox injections, and on every second visit, once a year, they receive a Restylane touch-up. Other procedures are done as needed, including radiofrequency treatment and CO_2 *laser resurfacing* (which produces more dramatic results than IPL, but also requires recovery time).

The final component of the program is a good home-care regimen—including regular use of a sun block to prevent UV damage, as well as products that speed up the turnover of the skin cells. (In my practice, I use the Obagi line of skin-care products. These products are powerful and use must be supervised by a physician who is appropriately trained. To find such a physician, visit *www.obagi.com.*)

BOTTOM LINE: Women and men who follow this innovative skin rejuvenation program not only have great-looking skin, but also have at their disposal a less-invasive alternative to cosmetic surgery as they get older.

■

REPORT #25

FREE BENEFITS FOR SENIORS

Source: **The National Council on the Aging,** 300 D St. SW, Washington, DC 20024.

The Web site *www.benefitscheckup.org* is an on-line service which identifies more than 1,300 government and private benefit programs for those age 55 or over.

Users fill out a confidential questionnaire and receive a personalized report listing programs and benefits they may be eligible to receive, along with detailed descriptions of programs and contact information.

■

REPORT #26

THE ULTIMATE TAX-FREE ESTATE PLAN

Source: **Martin M. Shenkman, CPA and attorney,** specializing in trusts and estates in New York City and Teaneck, NJ. He is author of more than 30 books, including *The Complete Living Trusts Program* (John Wiley & Sons). His Web site is *www.laweasy.com.*

Too many people mistakenly assume that trusts are only for the fabulously wealthy and not for those with just a family home, a company pension and a life insurance policy. But even these people can benefit substantially from trusts.

REASON: Trusts save thousands of dollars in gift and estate taxes and provide a way to manage assets when the original owners are no longer available. They also can protect assets from creditors and malpractice suits.

Trusts need to be set up properly if they are to be effective, so be sure to consult a knowledgeable attorney. Here are five basic types of trusts and what they can do for you.

1. LIFE INSURANCE TRUST...

Let's say you own your home and have some modest investments, a pension and a $500,000 life insurance policy. If your children are the beneficiaries of this insurance policy, your family could owe the government hundreds of thousands of dollars in additional estate taxes.

REASON: Life insurance proceeds, while not subject to federal income tax, are considered part of your taxable estate and are subject to federal estate tax—up to 46% in 2006.

SOLUTION: Create an irrevocable life insurance trust which will own the policy and receive the cash payout upon the policy owner's death. **THERE ARE SEVERAL BENEFITS TO DOING THIS...**

• *Income for the beneficiaries.* The irrevocable life insurance trust can be structured so that your survivors receive some or all of the annual income generated by the trust. The survivors can even receive the principal—subject to certain restrictions.

• *Avoidance of estate taxes.* If it's properly structured, such a trust ensures that insurance proceeds escape taxation in your estate as well as the estate of your surviving spouse. In addition, because the proceeds are not included in your taxable estate or your spouse's taxable estate, they are not part of the public record and escape publicity. They also are not affected by probate costs.

• *Protection of assets.* The trust protects insurance proceeds from creditors and malpractice actions.

• *Reliable management.* By naming a family member and an outsider, such as a bank or accountant, to manage the trust assets, you eliminate the problem of relying on inexperienced or incapable beneficiaries to handle the trust's money.

2. CREDIT SHELTER TRUST...

Even though the estate tax is repealed in 2010 no one can predict one's date of death. In the meantime, take advantage of tax-free exemption amounts.

The primary purpose of a credit shelter trust is to preserve the applicable estate-tax exemption that all individuals get in their estates.

Under the law, everyone can give away $12,000 to individuals in 2006, and a certain amount during his or her lifetime ($1 million), or upon death tax free ($2 million in 2006). Most couples own all of their property jointly and have wills in which the husband leaves everything to the wife and the wife leaves everything to the husband. This may not be the best arrangement.

REASON: Let's assume that a couple jointly owns an estate worth $4 million. When one of the spouses dies in 2006, there will be no estate tax because of the unlimited marital deduction. But when the second spouse dies a year later, the estate will owe nearly three quarters of a million or roughly one quarter of the estate in estate taxes.

SOLUTION: When your joint estate exceeds twice the applicable exemption amount, divide all the joint property equally between you and your spouse. For example, transform a joint brokerage account into two separate accounts with half the assets in each. Then create a credit shelter trust under each spouse's will. The trust will allow the estate of each spouse to escape tax by taking maximum advantage of the applicable exemption amount assuming there are sufficient assets to fund the trust.

EXAMPLE: When the first spouse dies, the assets valued up to the applicable exemption amount go into a credit shelter trust for the benefit of the second spouse. (When the second spouse dies, those assets pass directly to the children or other heirs, with no estate tax.)

Whichever spouse survives can have the right to receive all the income produced by the trust. That spouse also has the right to take principal from the trust to maintain his or her standard of living. It's almost like having the assets in your own name.

IMPORTANT: It's not enough to just create the trust. Retitle your joint property in separate names so that, upon your death, the property can be transferred to the trust in order for it to save your family additional estate taxes.

3. QTIP TRUST...

A Qualified Terminable Interest Property (QTIP) trust defers taxes and helps families attain personal goals. Its aim is to ensure that, after a spouse's death, assets exceeding the applicable exemption amount pass first to the surviving spouse tax free and then to the individuals for whom they are ultimately intended.

BENEFIT: The trust is often used with second marriages to provide lifelong support for a current spouse. Then, after the second spouse's death, the QTIP funnels assets to the children from the first marriage.

Under this arrangement, your current spouse receives all of the income annually from the trust for life. Even though your spouse's interest in the trust property terminates upon death, the initial transfer of property to the trust still qualifies for the unlimited marital deduction.

4. CHILDREN'S TRUST...

This trust is formulated to provide for your children and addresses a problem that occurs with gifts to children under the Uniform Gifts to Minors Act (UGMA) and Uniform Transfers to Minors Act (UTMA).

PROBLEM: Under UGMA and UTMA, once children reach age 18 or 21 (depending on the state in which they reside), they can do whatever they wish with the money in their custodial accounts. If they want to use it to support a commune or buy a sports car instead of finishing college, there's nothing you can do about it.

SOLUTION: By transferring assets to a children's trust, such as a Crummey trust, the trustee can determine how the money in the trust is to be used and how much the child can receive.

5. GRANDPARENTS' TRUST...

This trust is similar to the children's trust, except that the grandparents establish it to help pay for their grandchildren's college expenses.

A separate trust can be created for each grandchild. There is a $12,000 per grandparent limit on the amount that can be placed gift-tax-free in each trust in 2006 (the $12,000 may be adjusted for inflation in the future).

As with a children's trust, the trust document and the trustee define how much money can be used for which purposes.

IMPORTANT: Avoid setting up a single trust that names more than one grandchild as a beneficiary. Otherwise, you will run into the expensive generation-skipping transfer (GST) tax, which, in many instances, applies to transfers of more than $2 million in 2006.

NOTE: There have been sweeping changes to the GST so consult a tax expert.

■

REPORT #27

TOP 10 BIG MISTAKES WHEN PLANNING YOUR ESTATE

Source: **Martin M. Shenkman, CPA and attorney,** specializing in trusts and estates in New York City and Teaneck, NJ. He is author of more than 30 books, including *The Complete Living Trusts Program* (John Wiley & Sons). His Web site is *www.laweasy.com*.

An estate plan should be a clear roadmap, one that guides your assets to your chosen beneficiaries with a minimum of time and expense.

That's what it should be, but too often it's not. Inaction and planning blunders can result in disaster for your loved ones.

CONSIDER WHAT COULD HAPPEN: Your estate could fall into the wrong hands...the IRS could end up with far more than its fair share...or your heirs could battle endlessly.

None of this will happen to your estate as long as you avoid the most frequent and damaging planning mistakes...

1. *Not having a will.* If you die without one, your assets will be divided according to state law, which may not be the disposition you desire. For example, in some states, your spouse and children split your estate.

2. *Focusing solely on taxes.* To many people, estate planning is synonymous with tax planning. They reason that since the federal estate tax exemption is currently $2 million—they won't owe estate tax and don't need to do any planning.

The size of your estate—taxes or no taxes—should never determine whether you have a comprehensive plan. Most estate-related family disputes are not even about money. They occur because people ignore the human element of estate planning.

HERE ARE SOME EXAMPLES...

• Heirs may squabble over furniture, inexpensive jewelry, family photographs, etc.—things you might never think they would fight over.

• You might name one child as executor, and inadvertently slight your other children no matter how the assets are divided up.

3. *Being mysterious.* It may make good TV drama, but there's usually nothing to be gained by keeping heirs totally in the dark about your intentions. Explain your choices to them, and specify your bequests. Give away heirlooms while you're alive—you'll get to see your heirs enjoying them, and they won't have to fight over them later. And, as we saw in the case of Terri Schiavo, it's vital to let your family know what you would want done if difficult medical decisions have to be made.

STRATEGY: Discussions with family are not legally binding. Neither are personal notes. Include your wishes in formal legal documents to prevent fights. Have a living will drafted stating your health-care wishes. Get a health-care proxy appointing an agent to make decisions.

4. *Failing to update beneficiary designations.* Life insurance policies, retirement accounts, payable-on-death (POD) accounts set up at banks and with brokerage firms, and certain other assets will pass to the beneficiaries you have named in the accounts' paperwork, no matter what it says in your will. You should check periodically to be sure your beneficiary choices in these accounts are current.

After a divorce, for example, you probably won't want your ex-spouse to be the beneficiary of your life insurance or your IRA.

5. *Relying on outdated documents.* Assets change, families change and the laws change. All of your estate-planning documents—will, trusts, letters of instruction to an executor, power of attorney—should be reviewed at least once every three years...and anytime a relevant law changes.

EXAMPLE: A common strategy has been to leave the amount of the estate tax exemption to a bypass trust for the children and the balance of the estate to the surviving spouse, since spousal bequests are automatically tax free.

The estate tax exemption is scheduled to rise, though, so such a plan may leave too much to the kids and too little to your spouse.

6. *Naming the wrong executor.* After your death, your executor will become the quarterback of your estate plan, responsible for handling all the assets that transfer under your will.

TRAP: If you name your spouse, he/she might be too overcome by your death to function well. Similarly, it may not be practical to name your son, who lives across the country.

STRATEGY: Name a young relative who lives nearby, someone who is well-organized and detail-oriented. If you think that your spouse's feelings will be hurt, designate such a person coexecutor along with your spouse.

Whoever you name, make sure to ask him if he is willing to serve. Name two or three backups, too, in case your first choice is unable or unwilling to act.

7. *Making things difficult for your executor.* If your financial papers are scattered everywhere, handling your estate will be more difficult and time-consuming. Valuable assets (such as life insurance policies) may be overlooked.

STRATEGY: Keep copies of your documents in one place, such as a looseleaf binder or folder. Write on each copy where the original is located—and let your executor know where the originals can be found—such as with your lawyer, who may have your original will. Simplify things for your executor by consolidating accounts with one bank, one broker, one mutual fund company, one insurance company, etc., to the extent that is practical.

8. *Improper use of joint ownership.* As you grow older, you might want to add the name of a relative, such as your daughter, to your bank or brokerage accounts. This joint owner could write checks, handle investments and so on, if you become unable to manage your own affairs.

TRAP: Your co-owner will automatically inherit that asset, freezing out all other heirs no matter what's in your will.

STRATEGY: Instead of joint ownership, give to your trusted friend or relative a durable power of attorney over your accounts. This person will be able to handle your affairs if need be, yet your will shall remain fully in effect.

If you want one younger relative to be able just to write checks for you, name him as joint owner of a checking account where relatively modest sums are maintained.

9. *Underestimating the size of your estate.* Despite all the talk of estate tax repeal, the federal estate tax is still on the books...and most states are *increasing* their estate taxes.

If you leave a sizable estate, chances are that your heirs will owe some tax.

TRAP: Even if you don't think of yourself as rich, if you die while owning real estate, life insurance policies and a retirement account, you may be in estate tax territory.

STRATEGY: Some planning can help reduce the tax burden you'll leave to your loved ones.

EXAMPLE: In 2006, you can give up to $12,000 per year to any number of recipients with no tax consequences. That number will increase in future years with inflation.

You may also want to arrange for insurance on your life to be purchased in a trust if your estate will need cash to cover an expected estate tax bill. Talk to your financial adviser.

10. *Not coordinating advisers.* Good estate planning involves a variety of skills. Having all your legal documents (will, trusts, etc.) in order may not guarantee a sound estate plan if your life insurance is not handled properly. Similarly, you might need a tax adviser to see if tax planning is necessary and a financial planner to handle your investments.

KEY: Make sure all of your advisers know about each other —and about your entire estate plan—so they can work with each other to ensure a happy ending.

■

REPORT #28

TAKE YOUR CASH NOW, PAY NO PENALTY

Source: **James Blinka, CPA,** tax partner, BDO Seidman, LLP, Two Plaza E., 330 E. Kilbourne Ave., Milwaukee, WI 53202.

Anyone who withdraws money from an IRA or other tax-deferred retirement plan will owe income tax, assuming the account was funded with deductible contributions.

In most situations, you will also owe a 10% penalty tax on withdrawals before age 59½. For instance, if you withdraw $10,000 at age 54 (and don't qualify for an exception to the penalty), you would have to pay a $1,000 penalty.

But there are some exceptions to the early withdrawal penalty. If you really must take an early withdrawal, use one of the following methods to avoid the 10% penalty tax bite.

UNIVERSAL EXCEPTIONS...

The following exceptions apply to all tax-deferred retirement plans...

• *Death.* If you inherit a retirement account, you won't face the 10% penalty. That's true no matter how old you are (and no matter how old the participant was at the time of death).

• *Disability.* Again, the 10% penalty does not apply if you cannot work and need to make a withdrawal.

How can you prove to the IRS that you are disabled? In most cases, you should be receiving disability checks from Social Security or from an insurance policy.

SMART 1040 STRATEGY: Attach an explanation to your tax return, clearly stating that you are receiving disability benefits and that the 10% penalty should not apply.

• *Medical bills.* The 10% penalty will not apply to any money spent for deductible medical expenses in excess of 7.5% of your adjusted gross income (AGI).

• *Substantially equal periodic payments (SEPPs).* Avoid the 10% penalty by withdrawing annual amounts based on your life expectancy. These payments must continue for at least five years or until age 59½, whichever comes later.

CAUTION: If you don't maintain the SEPPs until the later of five years or until age 59½, you will owe the 10% penalty tax on all withdrawals, retroactively.

EMPLOYER-SPONSORED PLANS...

The following two exceptions to the 10% early withdrawal penalty apply only to withdrawals from 401(k)s, profit-sharing plans and other qualified retirement plans.

• *Separation from service.* If you leave your employer, you can take money from your retirement account and not pay a penalty.

REQUIREMENT: The separation must occur no earlier than the year you reach age 55.

• *Qualified domestic relations orders (QDROs).* In a divorce or marital separation, a QDRO is an order to the plan administrator to transfer a portion of one spouse's account to the other spouse. Such a transfer won't be subject to taxes. But subsequent withdrawals from an employer-sponsored plan under a QDRO before age 59½ will be subject to a penalty.

IMPLICATION: You can give or receive alimony or child support from an employer-sponsored retirement plan, penalty free, as long as those payments are required by a QDRO.

Don't take the money out of a plan and then give it to your spouse. The IRS will look harshly on that approach, applying income tax under the theory that you took a distribution. Money should go directly to the beneficiary of the QDRO, as required.

IRA EXCEPTIONS...

The separation-from-service and QDRO exceptions do not apply to early distributions from IRAs. **ON THE OTHER HAND, THERE ARE ESCAPE HATCHES THAT ARE ONLY FOR IRAs...**

• *Higher education.* Distributions from IRAs for post-high-school expenses are exempt from the 10% penalty.

ELIGIBLE EXPENSES: Tuition, room and board, fees, books, supplies and necessary equipment.

These qualifying expenses can be used to pay for your education or that of your spouse, your children or your grandchildren.

• *Health insurance.* After you are out of work for 12 consecutive weeks, you can take money from an IRA to keep your health insurance in force, penalty free.

After you're back at work, you won't owe a penalty on IRA withdrawals used to pay health insurance premiums for the next 60 days.

• *Purchasing a first home.* You may take penalty-free withdrawals up to $10,000 for a first-time home purchase.

REQUIRED: You cannot have had an ownership interest in a residence during the previous two years. The $10,000 is a lifetime limit.

ROTH IRAs...

If you're withdrawing money before age 59½ from a Roth IRA converted from a traditional IRA, you'll owe the penalty on the amount that is attributable to your earnings inside the Roth IRA, but not to your original contributions.

EXCEPTIONS: Death, disability and first-time home buyer up to $10,000.

THE SEPP SOLUTION...

Some of the exceptions listed above (death, disability, divorce) apply only in specific circumstances. However, IRA owners can make use of the SEPP exception at any time. Participants in other plans can use SEPPs after separation from service.

SEPP rules are so flexible that you can take out almost any amount needed, penalty free, as long as your account balance is large enough. THREE METHODS PERMITTED BY THE IRS...

• *Life expectancy.* You withdraw money based on your life expectancy, according to the IRS tables. For instance, if your life expectancy is 40 years, you would calculate ¼₀ (2.5%) of your plan balance and withdraw that much each year.

• *Amortization.* You calculate that your initial plan balance will grow by a reasonable rate, perhaps 6% or 7% each year. The higher the assumed rate is, the greater the penalty-free withdrawals permitted. This method allows much higher withdrawals than the life-expectancy method.

• *Annuitization.* This complicated calculation, incorporating annuity factors and present values, allows you to withdraw a bit more than with the amortization method.

EXAMPLE: You have a $600,000 IRA and you wish to withdraw $2,500 per month. However, if the SEPP rules (amortization method) require that you withdraw $3,750 per month from a $600,000 IRA, you'd be paying tax on an unneeded $1,250 a month.

SOLUTION: Split your $600,000 IRA into a $400,000 IRA and a $200,000 IRA, tax free. Then take distributions from the $400,000 IRA, pulling out the $2,500 per month that you need, using the amortization method. In your other $200,000 IRA, you can continue the tax-free buildup.

REPORT #29

IRA ROLLOVERS MADE EASY

Source: **Robert S. Keebler, CPA, MST,** partner, Virchow, Krause & Co., LLP, 1400 Lombardi Ave., Green Bay, WI 54304. Mr. Keebler is author of *A CPA's Guide to Making the Most of the New IRA* (AICPA).

Your IRA may wind up being one of your largest assets, if not the largest. You probably will not accumulate a huge amount from $4,000 or $5,000 annual contributions (the current limits, depending on your age).

However, money in an employer-sponsored retirement plan can be rolled over to an IRA when you leave that employer, maintaining the tax deferral.

KEY: Such rollovers can put you in control of a six- or seven-figure investment portfolio. Making the right moves with your rollover can be vital to your financial future. **BUT IT'S IMPORTANT TO AVOID THESE MISTAKES...**

MISTAKE: Taking cash instead of doing a rollover when you change jobs. You may change jobs several times during your career. Often, you'll leave a company where you've participated in a 401(k) or similar retirement plan. In each case, you can roll your account balance into an IRA. Even modest amounts can become meaningful, after numerous years of tax-deferred buildup, when combined this way.

TRAP: If you simply take a cash payout from the plan, you'll owe income tax, and a 10% penalty if you're under age 55. Being human, you might spend what's left, leaving you short of retirement funds.

MISTAKE: Keeping your money in your former employer's plan. Many companies permit you to keep your money in their 401(k) plans, even after you leave. Some people think a company plan has no or very low fees, or that the investment selections have been carefully screened, so they decide to leave their money behind.

REALITY: Employer-sponsored plans often have high fees. You may well cut your costs with a self-directed IRA.

Moreover, some 401(k) plans offer good investment choices, but many of them are filled with mediocre funds in only a few asset classes.

KEY: With a rollover IRA, you have a virtually unlimited menu of investments. You can spread your wealth cost-effectively among top funds for large-company stocks, real estate stocks, international stocks, various types of bonds, etc.

MISTAKE: Keeping your accounts apart. Over time, if you have left three or four jobs, you may have three or four old 401(k) plans. Plus, you might have an IRA to which you've made annual contributions.

TRAP: With the puzzle pieces scattered around, you're making it difficult to put together a cohesive plan. You are more likely to wind up with an unbalanced portfolio, vulnerable to adverse market moves.

EXAMPLE: At each of your jobs, you have directed 401(k) contributions into growth funds that are heavy in technology stocks. You might not realize that your retirement fund is so exposed to a downturn in one market sector.

If you combine all of those tax-deferred accounts into one IRA, record keeping will be simpler. You can easily see what you've got and manage a unified portfolio.

LOOPHOLE: The law now permits you to combine all of your tax-deferred accounts, including IRAs to which you've made annual contributions, into one rollover IRA. Combining all of your tax-deferred accounts into one rollover IRA can help you coordinate your entire portfolio for greater tax efficiency.

EXAMPLE: You want to have a 10% portfolio allocation to real estate investment trusts (REITs) and real estate mutual funds. In a rollover IRA, these securities' high dividend payouts won't be subject to immediate taxation.

Concurrently, growth stocks that pay no dividends can be held in a taxable account, where any appreciation eventually will be favorably taxed as long-term capital gain.

MISTAKE: Neglecting estate planning. If you name someone other than your spouse a beneficiary of your retirement account, you have another reason to execute a rollover.

Most employer plans call for an immediate payout to a nonspouse beneficiary. Generally, all the money must be withdrawn (and taxed) right away, or within a few years.

LOOPHOLE: That's not as much of a problem with an IRA. A nonspouse beneficiary can stretch out IRA distributions over his/her life expectancy, enjoying valuable tax deferral.

MISTAKE: Rolling over employer stock. In some situations, a partial rollover may be a wise move. That's especially true if you hold a great deal of appreciated employer stock in your account.

LOOPHOLE: Such stock can be pulled out of your plan entirely—as opposed to being rolled over—when you leave the company. (Some plans permit in-service withdrawals, after a certain age.) Under the Tax Code, you'll owe tax only on the shares' value when they were contributed to your account.

EXAMPLE: You're retiring with $500,000 in your company plan, of which $300,000 is in company stock. Those shares were worth $50,000 when they went into your account.

You can pull the company shares out of the plan and owe tax on only $50,000. The other $250,000—the net unrealized appreciation, or NUA—will be untaxed until you sell the shares, and then the favorable capital gains rate will apply.

In the meantime, the other $200,000 in your employer plan can be rolled over to an IRA.

TRAP: In the above example, if you do a complete rollover, all of your gains will be taxed as ordinary income at withdrawal. You could wind up paying 35% to the IRS instead of 15% on capital gains.

If the stock is worth less now than when you got it, it makes sense to do a complete rollover.

MISTAKE: Taking distributions yourself. If you decide on an IRA rollover, full or partial, ask that the money be sent directly from your employer to your IRA in a "trustee-to-trustee" transfer. If you receive any funds yourself, your employer must withhold 20%.

TRAP: The money withheld will be subject to income tax unless you make up the shortfall out of your own pocket. You may owe a 10% early withdrawal penalty, too.

EXAMPLE: John Parker, age 48, changes jobs and asks for his $400,000 balance in the company plan to be paid to him. His company withholds $80,000 (20%) and sends him a check for $320,000.

RESULT: Parker has 60 days to deposit $400,000 into an IRA, completing the rollover. If he puts the $320,000 check into the account, he will pick up $80,000 worth of taxable income. He is under age 55, so he'll also owe an $8,000 (10%) penalty on the amount that's considered withdrawn.

BETTER WAY: In a trustee-to-trustee transfer, no withholding is required. You can maintain full tax deferral and avoid the 10% penalty.

■

REPORT #30

THE INSTANT PENSION PLAN

Source: **Stacy L. Schaus, CFP,** practice leader for personal finance at Hewitt Associates, a global human resources consulting firm in Lincolnshire, IL.

In the past, retirees could rely on pensions and Social Security to replace most of their preretirement income. A 401(k) plan or IRA and personal savings provided additional support.

Today, with fewer companies providing pension plans, nonpension resources often are the sole support. Unfortunately, 401(k)s don't guarantee a steady income stream. **TO ENSURE THAT RETIREES WILL NOT OUTLIVE THEIR SAVINGS, MOST NEED TO CREATE THEIR OWN PENSIONS...**

HOW IT WORKS...

You can simulate your own pension plan by purchasing an immediate annuity. In exchange for your lump-sum payment, an insurance company agrees to provide a stable, guaranteed income every month for the remainder of your life.

There is no right or wrong age at which you should purchase an immediate annuity. Consider buying one when you need to replace or supplement your income. **SMART STRATEGY...**

• *Ask whether your employer offers an annuity option* via your retirement plan—it may offer a more generous payout than an annuity you would purchase privately.

• *Compare annuity payout rates* and request free reports at *www.immediateannuities.com* (800-872-6684). There can be big differences among providers.

ALSO: Whether you're buying through your employer or on your own, make sure the company's claims-paying ability is rated A+ or better by A.M. Best (908-439-2200, *www.ambest.com*) or AA by Standard & Poor's (212-438-2400, *www.sandp.com*).

• *Factor in expenses.* Compare net results or monthly income amounts from different providers.

ANNUITY OPTIONS...

Your monthly annuity income depends on your age, the size of your lump-sum payment and any special features you choose. For instance, for a $100,000 straight life annuity purchased directly from a financial institution, a typical 65-year-old male could get about $650 a month. (Purchasing one via an employer might generate a higher payout.)

Payments from a straight life annuity stop when you die, whether death occurs in the first year of the annuity or 30 years later. In the example above, the retiree would get $7,800 a year and so would have to live about 13 years to recover his initial investment without interest. **THERE ARE FEATURES YOU CAN ADD THAT ADJUST FOR THESE AND OTHER UNCERTAINTIES...**

• *Life income for a fixed period.* If you die soon after the annuity payouts begin, your beneficiaries continue to receive payments for the period contracted—say, for 10 or 20 years. This feature will decrease the monthly payout—so, with a 20-year fixed period, the 65-year-old male in the example above and, subsequently, his beneficiaries, might receive a monthly payout of $550.

WHO SHOULD CHOOSE THIS OPTION: People who want expenses to be covered whether they are living or not, for an established period of time, possibly until other income sources kick in. This feature is not for people who want to ensure payment for the life of a coannuitant, such as a spouse.

• *Fixed period only.* This type of annuity pays income only for a specific length of time—for instance, exactly 10 years. This approach provides you with the highest monthly payout—for example, the 65-year-old male might receive a check for $950 every month for the 10 years.

WHO SHOULD CHOOSE THIS OPTION: Someone whose main concern is having income for a specific period and who knows that future income sources will be available after that period.

• *Cost-of-living rider.* If you're concerned that inflation will erode the value of your annuity payment over time, you may want to shop for a provider that will build in a cost-of-living adjustment. Some insurers allow you to increase your payout by, say, 3% each year. Others base increases on changes in the Consumer Price Index. Of course, this feature will mean a reduced monthly payout at first, depending on the extent of the increase or inflation protection, but you'll come out ahead if you live long enough.

WHO SHOULD CHOOSE THIS OPTION: People who don't think they can hedge against inflation in less costly ways—for instance, by combining an immediate annuity with equity investments. Such a strategy can hedge against inflation effectively while maximizing current income.

• *Joint-and-survivor.* This annuity continues paying a percentage of income—typically, 50% to 100%—to your spouse or beneficiary after your death. The higher the percentage earmarked for your beneficiary and the younger he/she is, the smaller the monthly payout.

IMPORTANT: Seek advice from a fee-only adviser (not a commissioned salesperson) to determine the best approach. For instance, purchasing a life insurance policy along with an immediate annuity may be more tax efficient for your situation than a joint-and-survivor annuity.

Many of the above features can be combined, so it's critical to compare apples to apples when choosing an annuity.

WHEN TO BUY...

With interest rates headed higher, you may be concerned that now is not the best time to buy an annuity. It's true that higher interest rates may mean a higher annuity payout if you wait, but in the meantime, you might earn less on your cash than required to meet your needs.

If your income need is immediate but you are concerned about the level of interest rates, consider dollar cost averaging annuity purchases over the next two to three years and/or purchasing some inflation protection.

BEST STRATEGY: Consider buying an annuity now with some of your money to cover your fixed cash needs. Then invest the remainder of your savings for the longer term. You may rest more comfortably investing in stocks or other securities knowing that your fixed expenses will be covered. Don't forget to set aside some cash for emergencies and, if you wish, for your heirs.

Keep in mind that annuities aren't for everyone. If you can live comfortably on the income from your investments without worrying about exhausting your principal, then an annuity may not be appropriate. Seek the counsel of a trusted adviser to set up a retirement income strategy. Since purchase of an annuity is an irrevocable decision, it's critical for you to understand what you're buying and how it fits with your overall financial and estate plan.

■

TAXES

4

TAXES

REPORT #31

$1 MILLION TAX-FREE CASH
FOR YOUR KIDS

Source: **Irving L. Blackman, CPA,** founding partner, Blackman Kallick Bartel-stein, LLP, 10 S. Riverside Plaza, Chicago 60606, *www.taxsecretsofthewealthy.com.*

If you want to make a major bequest to a child or grandchild, the smart way to do it may be to use life insurance instead of a bequest of property.

Say you want to leave $1 million to a grandchild. First you need to have at least that much in assets—and, after you take into consideration federal and local estate taxes, you may need twice as much. Remember, federal estate tax isn't sched-uled to be repealed until 2010 and may never be—and state death taxes continue to apply.

Also, income earned on the assets is subject to income tax at top rates—and the assets are "tied up." You can't spend them *and* bequeath them, too.

If you wish to make several such bequests, these problems are multiplied.

ALTERNATIVE: Fund the bequest to the child with a $1 million life insurance policy held in a life insurance trust. **WHY...**

• *A properly structured trust will be estate tax free*—reducing the assets you need by as much as half and cutting the IRS out of the deal.

• *Investment income earned within the insurance policy will be tax free.*

• *The dollar cost is very low* since the value of the policy is leveraged through tax savings.

EXAMPLE: A married couple, both age 60, find they can buy a $1 million second-to-die life insurance policy (that pays on the death of the survivor) for an annual premium of about $13,000 a year for 15 years. They place the policy in a life insurance trust benefiting a child. Policy premiums are gift tax free, due to the couple's annual joint gift tax exclusion ($24,000 in 2006).

PAYOFF: The child will receive $1 million tax free at a maximum cash cost to the couple of only $195,000. And the after-tax cost may be as much as 50% less, as the $195,000 is removed from the parents' taxable estate.

■

REPORT #32

HOW TO EARN INVISIBLE INCOME THE IRS CAN'T TOUCH

Source: **Edward Mendlowitz, CPA,** shareholder, WithumSmith+Brown, 120 Albany St., New Brunswick, NJ 08901. He is the author of various books on taxes, including *IRA Distributions: What You Should Know* (Practical Programs).

Not all of the money you receive is taxable income, even though the IRS might like you to think it is.

GAIN ON THE SALE OF YOUR HOME...

You're not taxed on gain up to $250,000 ($500,000 on a joint return) from the sale of your principal residence. You qualify for this exclusion if you owned and used the home for two out of five years before the date of the sale, regardless of your age.

LIFE INSURANCE PROCEEDS...

The beneficiary receives the proceeds of life insurance policies free of tax. However, the decedent's estate may be liable for estate tax on the proceeds.

GIFTS AND INHERITANCES...

You do not pay income tax on money or property you receive as a gift or inheritance. Any gift tax owed is the responsibility of the person who gave the gift. In the case of an inheritance, federal estate tax is paid by the decedent's estate, not by the beneficiaries.

If you inherit property that has increased in value, such as the family home, you receive it at its stepped-up estate value. This enables you to avoid tax on the gain. When you sell the property, you use its stepped-up value, rather than the original cost, to calculate your taxable gain—another big benefit.

BORROWED MONEY...

You can borrow up to $50,000 from your company pension plan tax free.

TRAP: If a debt you owe is canceled, the amount of debt forgiven might become taxable income to you.

GRANTS FOR EDUCATION...

Scholarships and fellowship grants are tax free—provided you are a degree candidate and the money is used strictly for tuition, fees, books, supplies and required equipment. (Grants for room and board are taxable.)

EMPLOYEE AWARDS...

Awards of tangible personal property (not cash) for length of service or safety achievements—up to $400 per employee or $1,600 provided the employer has a qualified plan—are tax free. (Awards for suggestions to an employer are generally taxable.)

DAMAGES...

Any damages received in a lawsuit due to personal physical injury or sickness are tax free.

ROLLOVERS...

No taxes are payable on a lump-sum payout from a company pension plan directly transferred into an IRA or another qualified plan within 60 days.

PROPERTY SETTLEMENTS...

Settlements between spouses in a divorce are not taxable to the recipient. However, the recipient does take over the tax cost (basis) in the property and will be taxed on any gain when the property is sold.

CHILD SUPPORT AND ALIMONY...

Child-support payments are tax free to the recipient. Alimony is generally taxable, but it can be tax free if both spouses agree.

MUNICIPAL BOND INTEREST...

Generally, the interest is exempt from federal income tax and sometimes from state and local tax as well.

EXCEPTION: Interest from certain "private activity" municipal bonds is subject to the Alternative Minimum Tax (AMT). Also, municipal bond interest is taken into account in figuring your income level to determine whether any of your Social Security benefits are taxable.

RETURN-OF-CAPITAL DIVIDENDS...

Some companies pay dividends that are considered a return on your investment in the company. These are wholly or partially tax free. However, your tax cost in the stock has to be reduced by the amount of untaxed dividends.

LIFE INSURANCE POLICY DIVIDENDS...

These are generally considered a partial return of the premiums you paid and are not taxable. You don't have to pay tax on these dividends until they exceed the accumulated premiums paid for the policy.

ANNUITY PAYMENTS...

The part of an annuity payment that represents the return of your investment in the annuity contract is not taxed. Pension and IRA distributions that represent any non-tax-deductible contributions are also not taxed.

EDUCATION SAVINGS BONDS...

Interest on US Series EE and I savings bonds that were issued after December 31, 1989, is tax free to many taxpayers if the bonds are later redeemed to pay for education expenses.

LIMITS: This exclusion is not available for taxpayers with income in excess of certain annually determined amounts.

ALSO TAX FREE...

- *Workers' compensation.*
- *Social Security payments*—provided your income is less than $32,000 if married filing jointly, or $25,000 if filing singly.
- *Federal income-tax refunds.* (However, any interest the IRS pays on a late refund is taxable.)
- *State income-tax refunds,* provided that you did not itemize deductions on your federal tax return for the previous year. If, however, you itemized your deductions for the year, your state refund is taxable. State refunds are not taxable if you were subject to the AMT the previous year and got no tax benefit for your state tax payments.
- *Disability payments* from any accident or health insurance policies paid for by the taxpayer are generally not taxable. But they're usually taxable if your employer paid the premiums.
- *Foreign-earned income.* The first $82,400 of salary earned in another country in 2006 is excluded from US tax if you were a resident of that country for the entire tax year. Some of your housing expenses are also excluded from US tax.
- *Certain fringe benefits from your employer.*

EXAMPLES: Health and accident insurance, pension plans, up to $50,000 of life insurance coverage, child- and dependent-care expenses, adoption assistance, meal money, employee discounts and transit passes not exceeding $100 per month.

- *Reimbursed medical expenses* that are not claimed as itemized deductions.
- *Reimbursed travel and entertainment expenses* that you adequately account for to your employer (unless the reimbursement is included on your W-2 form).
- *The amounts received for insurance reimbursement* up to the amount of your original cost for the property that was lost or damaged.

AMT ALERT...

The AMT prevents the taxpayers who benefit from special credits and deductions from paying too little or no taxes. You may have to pay the AMT if your taxable income with adjustments in 2006 is above a certain level ($62,550 for married filing jointly and $42,500 for single or head of household). These figures are not adjusted annually for inflation, and are set to decline after 2006 unless Congress takes action.

■

REPORT #33

PAY ZERO CAPITAL GAINS FOR LIFE

Source: **Robert S. Keebler, CPA, MST,** partner, Virchow, Krause & Co., LLP, 1400 Lombardi Ave., Green Bay, WI 54304. Mr. Keebler is author of *A CPA's Guide to Making the Most of the New IRA* (AICPA).

In recent years, investors have learned the risks of holding a "concentrated portfolio." If most or all of your investment holdings were in Merck or Marsh & McLennan or, even worse, Enron, unexpected events would have suddenly put a whopping dent in your net worth.

Diversification reduces your dependence on one stock. To spread your risks, you can sell a large portion of your main holding and reinvest in other companies or mutual funds.

TRAP: If your concentrated position consists of highly appreciated shares held in a taxable account, selling will result in a huge tax bill.

EXAMPLE: You invested $10,000 in The Home Depot many years ago. Now that position is worth $500,000, a large chunk of your net worth. Although you are still upbeat on its prospects, you want to sell the shares to reduce your exposure to one stock. However, selling would trigger a $490,000 capital gain, at a 15% tax rate, and a $73,500 tax obligation. Depending on where you live, state and local tax might drive the total tax bill over $100,000.

CHARITABLE THOUGHTS...

One way to solve this problem is to donate your stock to a charitable remainder trust (CRT) you've created.

BENEFITS: You would get a large up-front tax deduction. The CRT could sell the shares, tax free, and invest the full amount in a diversified portfolio. (You will be able to direct the investments if you are a trustee of the CRT.) You and perhaps your spouse could receive a lifelong income stream from the CRT, without worrying about reliance on one stock.

DRAWBACKS: A CRT may be costly to create and maintain. A CRT probably would have to be worth six figures to justify the expense. Ultimately, the CRT assets will pass to charity, not to your heirs, which might be an undesirable result, as far as you're concerned.

OPTION PLAYS...

If a CRT strategy doesn't appeal to you, another approach is to buy "put" options. Put options on many widely traded stocks are available to individual investors.

HOW IT WORKS: A put option gives the holder the right to sell a particular stock for a set price ("strike price") at a specified time.

KEY: If a "European-style" put is purchased, it may not be exercised until the put expires. A two- or three-year put will, therefore, provide tax deferral (you do not pay tax until you sell the stock) as well as downside protection because the put locks in a minimum selling price.

During those two or three years, other tax-planning measures may be implemented. You might, for example, harvest capital losses on other assets. Such losses can be accumulated to offset gains—which you may then decide to take on your concentrated position.

EXAMPLE: You own 5,000 shares of company ABC's stock, now trading at $100 per share. You purchase a put option to sell all 5,000 shares at $90 per share on March 21, 2008.

If the stock price is more than $90 per share on that date, you can allow your put option to expire unexercised. Conversely, should the stock price fall below $90 per share, you can exercise your put option and sell your shares.

OUTCOME: You retain unlimited upside potential for ABC, yet you limit your downside risk to $90 per share, a 10% drop from current pricing.

PUTTING ON A COLLAR...

But be careful—buying a put option can be expensive. If it is not exercised, you'll have spent a sizable amount of money for no tangible result.

EXAMPLE: You own 10,000 shares of ABC at $50 a share for a total of $500,000. You purchase 10,000 puts at $3 a share for a cost of $30,000. If the price of the stock stays above $3/share—so you don't exercise the puts—you've lost $30,000 as a result of purchasing them.

STRATEGY: Sell a call option for your ABC shares, too.

HOW IT WORKS: A call option gives the holder the right to buy a particular stock for a set price at a specified time.

EXAMPLE: When you buy a put, as above, you also can sell a call on your ABC shares, at, say, $110 per share.

RESULT: The money you receive for selling the call might offset most or all of the money you pay for the put, depending on market conditions.

You'll wind up with the prospect of selling ABC to the owner of the call, if the stock goes above $110 a share, or using your put option to sell ABC at $90, if the stock falls below that price.

KEY: You've now limited your risk as well as your profit potential in the stock. In the language of Wall Street, you have a "collar," between $90 and $110 per share.

If the sale proceeds from selling the call completely offset the cost of buying the put, you have a "cashless collar."

If either option is exercised, and you sell the stock, you may realize a large taxable gain. For one technique to deal with this gain, see the margin strategy below.

ON THE MARGIN...

Your collar position is considered a safe asset, so brokerage firms will lend against it. Relatively low-cost "margin" loans will be available for up to 50% of the value of the underlying stock.

EXAMPLE: With a collar on $500,000 worth of ABC shares, as above, you can borrow up to $250,000 at an interest rate pegged to the broker's rate.

That $250,000, in turn, can be used to invest in a diverse portfolio.

STRATEGY: If you invest in a variety of stocks, you'll probably have winners as well as losers. Winners can be held for untaxed appreciation, while losers can be sold to accumulate capital losses.

Ultimately, when you sell your ABC shares and recognize long-term gains, the harvested losses can help to offset the tax on those gains.

BOTTOM LINE: If ABC winds up within the $90 to $110 collar when the options expire, you can then enter into another cashless collar.

If the stock goes below $90 or above $110, you'll sell your shares and use the proceeds to repay the margin loan.

OUTCOME: After a sale and loan repayment, you'll hold a diversified portfolio of stocks so you no longer bear the risk of a concentrated portfolio.

LOOPHOLE: Although interest continues to accrue while the loan is outstanding, it's likely that this interest will be tax deductible as an investment interest expense.

TAX TRAPS...

If you enter into a cashless collar, as described above, you must be wary of some potential tax pitfalls...

• *Avoid a "constructive sale."* If you set your collar too tightly, the IRS may argue that you have virtually sold the underlying stock because you have practically eliminated any potential future gain or loss.

EXAMPLE: With ABC trading at $100, you buy a put for $98 and sell a call at $102.

RESULT: You may be taxed as if you had actually sold the underlying stock when you entered into the option transactions.

STRATEGY: In general, there should be at least a 20% difference between the put and call option strike prices.

EXAMPLE: With a $90 put and a $110 call, as illustrated above, the $20 difference is 22% of the $90 put price. This probably will be sufficient to avoid a constructive sale.

• *Wait for long-term treatment.* Whenever you enter into a transaction that substantially reduces your risk due to offsetting positions, as in the case of a collar, the holding period for capital gains purposes will depend on how long the underlying stock was previously held.

LONG OR SHORT: If the underlying stock had been held for more than one year, the capital gain would be long-term when the underlying stock is sold. If the underlying stock had been held for one year or less at the time the collar was entered into, the capital gain would be short-term.

TRAP: This short-term treatment would apply no matter when the collar expired. In addition, the previous holding period would be terminated and a new holding period would not start until the collar had expired.

Thus, you would have to hold the stock for more than a year, after the collar expired, to get favorable long-term capital gains treatment.

KEY: To avoid this trap, wait until your holding period is long-term before entering into an options collar.

■

REPORT #34

TAX FORM LOOPHOLES THE IRS DOESN'T WANT YOU TO KNOW

Source: **Edward Mendlowitz, CPA,** shareholder, WithumSmith+Brown, 120 Albany St., New Brunswick, NJ 08901. He is the author of various books on taxes, including *IRA Distributions: What You Should Know* (Practical Programs).

Most people simply try to get the numbers right when they fill out their tax returns. But there is a lot more to this. Making strategic decisions can save you money, and, if you're careful, can reduce the odds of an IRS audit. **CONSIDER THESE STRATEGIES...**

FOR INDIVIDUAL TAXPAYERS...

LOOPHOLE: Make a Section 83(b) election when exercising any unvested incentive stock options. The election has to be made within 30 days of the exercise and will lower your alternative minimum tax (AMT) liability.

Making a Section 83(b) election means you owe AMT—in the same year that you make the election—on the difference between the exercise price for the options and the fair market value of the shares.

If you don't make the election, the AMT is calculated on the difference between the price you pay for the options and the fair market value of the shares when they vest.

STRATEGY: If you expect the shares to increase substantially in value, exercise incentive stock options as soon as possible. That way, you minimize the difference between the exercise price and the shares' market value.

LOOPHOLE: File a gift tax return for gifts used to pay insurance premiums. File the return even though it is not legally required.

When you give money to a trust to pay insurance premiums, no gift tax return is required if you give no more than $12,000 in 2006 and no grandchildren are involved (as long as the recipient signs a "Crummey" letter, making the payment a gift of a present interest).

If the IRS determines in a subsequent estate tax audit that the letter was inadequate, no statute of limitations will have run out. The donor or his/her estate could be liable for tax on the gifts.

BETTER: Filing a gift tax return blocks the IRS from assessing taxes after the three-year statute of limitations runs out.

LOOPHOLE: Don't take valuation discounts on Form 709 for small gifts. When you take a valuation discount for a gift, you must check the box on the gift tax return and include full disclosure of the reasons for the discount.

If you don't take a discount, the box is not checked off and you will decrease the chances of an audit. You should compare the benefits of avoiding an audit with the higher gift valuation.

LOOPHOLE: Enter Form 1099 information on Schedules B and D of your tax return—even if it's wrong. The IRS crosschecks the totals that are shown on Schedules B and D—reflecting capital gains, dividends and interest income—with the amounts banks, brokers and other payors report on Forms 1099. If the amounts differ, an IRS notice is automatically generated.

IF THERE'S A MISTAKE ON A 1099: Enter the 1099 figure on your tax return. Then subtract the erroneous amount to end up with your real total. Attach an explanatory letter to your return.

LOOPHOLE: Make a tardy generation-skipping transfer election. In general, grandparents who set up trusts for grandchildren can take a $2 million lifetime exemption in 2006, adjusted for inflation, for their collective gifts. When Form 709 is filed on time, the value of the gift is determined when the gift (or transfer) was actually made. When you make a late election, the value is determined when you filed the late return and elected to offset the gift's value against the lifetime exemption.

So, making a post-April 15 election saves money when the value of the gift decreases after you make it, such as a whole-life insurance policy premium.

TRAP: If you don't make a timely election and the insured dies, the full face value of the policy's face could be considered a generation-skipping transfer, which could create an enormous tax bill.

LOOPHOLE: Keep the total of your money in foreign bank accounts below $10,000. You must file a Form TD F 90-22.1 when the aggregate of foreign bank accounts in which you hold money and accounts from which you have check-signing power (even though the money is not yours) exceeds $10,000. Filing the form opens the accounts up for IRS scrutiny.

FOR BUSINESS TAXPAYERS...

LOOPHOLE: Choose a low-audit business code number to put on the company's Schedule C. The IRS targets for audit certain types of businesses and industries. When your business could legitimately fit into more than one category, choose the business code number that is not on the IRS's hit list. For example, a car wash can possibly be called an auto service center.

LOOPHOLE: Attach an "election schedule" for a controlled group of corporations to the corporation's Form 1120. When you run a controlled group of corporations (more than one corporation under common ownership), you must attach to the business's tax return an election schedule that includes an apportionment plan for certain tax items (for example, the AMT exemption). Otherwise, the IRS automatically allocates all exemptions and the benefits of the lower tax brackets equally among all the companies in the group.

STRATEGY: When you have a controlled group that includes dormant and active businesses, allocate all the exemptions and tax breaks to the active business.

LOOPHOLE: Report a fair market value appraisal on Form 1120S when you switch your C corporation to an S corporation. This will reduce the taxes owed on any built-in gains.

Businesses that convert from C corporation to S corporation status must value the business's assets as of the date of the conversion. If assets are sold within 10 years, profits are realized as if the C status were still in effect to the extent of any built-in gains as of that date, that is, the S corporation pays the tax.

STRATEGY: When you get a preconversion *fair market value* appraisal, the valuation is generally lower than what the assets could be sold for, saving taxes if the assets are sold before the 10-year deadline.

■

REPORT #35

INTEREST EXPENSE DEDUCTIONS YOU NEVER KNEW EXISTED

Source: The late **Gail T. Winawer, CPA,** former managing director, American Express Tax and Business Services Inc., 1185 Avenue of the Americas, New York City 10036.

The best way to minimize the after-tax cost of borrowing is to maximize your deduction for interest expense. **FOLLOW THESE GUIDELINES...**

YOUR DEBT PORTFOLIO...

Start by reviewing your total borrowing and considering it in terms of a "debt portfolio."

OBJECTIVE: To allocate your total borrowing among different kinds of debt in the manner that gives you the biggest total interest deduction.

KEY: Money is "fungible"—no matter how you get it, you can use it for any purpose.

If you want to borrow to finance, say, a consumer purchase, it's not necessary to take out a consumer loan to do so. You can instead borrow to finance some expenditure of another kind—such as an investment or business purchase—and use the cash you save to purchase the consumer item.

RESULT: Both the amount you borrow and the amount that you spend are unchanged—but you increase your interest deduction by borrowing more money in a manner that produces deductible interest.

Going forward, adjust your debt portfolio by planning new borrowing to be of a type that generates deductible interest. Also—consider taking advantage of today's low rates to pay off old nondeductible debt, replacing it with new tax-favored financing.

PLANNING OPPORTUNITIES...

The best planning opportunities for generating interest deductions exist with mortgage interest, investment interest and business interest. College loan interest also is deductible, but the deduction is subject to so many restrictions that planning opportunities for it are limited.

Consumer interest—such as the interest charged on credit cards to finance consumer purchases—is not deductible. Seek to make it as small a part of your debt portfolio as possible.

The deduction rules to use in planning...

• *Mortgage interest* is deductible on up to $1 million of borrowing used to acquire or improve a residence.

The deduction can be divided up between two residences. If you have a vacation home, you can deduct mortgage interest for it as well as for your primary residence. If you have more than two residences, you can claim the deduction for your primary residence and the second residence of your choice—and you can change that choice each year.

In addition, interest is tax deductible on up to $100,000 of home-equity borrowing, regardless of the purpose for which the borrowed funds are used.

RULE: To generate deductible mortgage interest, a loan must be secured by a residence. It is not enough to use a loan to buy or improve a home, if the loan is not secured by the home.

• *Investment interest* is deductible up to the amount of your net investment income. That equals your investment income —including dividends, interest and short-term capital gains— minus your investment expenses.

Excess investment interest may be carried forward to be deducted in future years, without limitation.

TACTIC: If your investment interest expense exceeds investment income, one may elect to treat long-term capital gains as short-term gains and deduct investment income against them.

Doing so yields a current deduction rather than a deferred one—but the deduction produces tax savings at only a maximum 20% rate, instead of at higher ordinary tax rates.

RULE: To produce an interest deduction, borrowed funds must be used to purchase an investment and be traceable to it. If you commingle borrowed funds with other funds in your checking account, you may lose the deduction—so keep borrowed investment funds in a segregated account.

• *Business interest* is deductible without limit when incurred as a business expense and reported on your return's Schedule C.

You can have this tax deduction if you operate a business proprietorship either full time or as a sideline. If you are an owner of a pass-through entity such as an S corporation, limited liability company or partnership, you should borrow the funds yourself.

EXAMPLE OF DEBT PORTFOLIO PLANNING: Say you intend to purchase a $20,000 automobile for personal use. If you use an auto loan to do so, you will get no interest deduction. But you may be able to obtain an interest deduction by using a $20,000 home-equity loan to buy the vehicle or by borrowing to finance a $20,000 investment or business expenditure instead of paying cash—and using the cash saved to buy the car.

HOME BORROWING...

This may be your most powerful method of reducing interest cost. Deduction rules are generous, and home-secured loans often carry lower interest rates than other kinds of loans.

SOME OPPORTUNITIES...

• *Home-equity borrowing exceeding $100,000 is deductible as...*

• Business interest, if the borrowed funds are used for a business purpose.

• Investment interest, if borrowed funds can be traced to the purchase of an investment.

ADVANTAGES: By using a home as security for a business or investment loan, you may get a lower interest rate—or obtain funds you couldn't get at all otherwise.

• *Home-equity borrowing up to $100,000 can be used for any purpose.* You can use such loans to refinance expensive and nondeductible credit card debt, or to finance new consumer purchases.

CAUTION: Beware of paying down your home mortgage too quickly. Many home owners do prepay their mortgages to increase their financial security and reduce the total interest they will pay on the mortgage over the years. But by prepaying your mortgage, you may significantly reduce the total deductible borrowing available to you.

If you prepay a mortgage to the point that equity in your home is in excess of $100,000 (the maximum home-equity loan for which interest is deductible), you will not be able to borrow against the excess with deductible interest even if you need the money.

Your home mortgage may just be your least expensive debt after taxes. Other debt, such as credit card debt, may incur much higher rates and not be deductible.

BEST: When prepaying debt, start with your most costly debt first. Your home mortgage may be last on the list.

REFINANCING...

If you increase the amount of the loan outstanding when refinancing a home loan to take advantage of a lower interest rate, deductibility depends on the amount refinanced and how you use the proceeds. If the excess is used to substantially improve the home, it can be treated as acquisition debt (subject to the $1 million limit). If it is used for other purposes (such as to pay off credit card balances), it can be treated as home equity debt (up to the $100,000 limit). Interest on any excess amount is nondeductible.

EXAMPLE: You have a $300,000 mortgage balance on a home worth $575,000. When refinancing your mortgage to obtain a lower interest rate, you increase the balance to $450,000 and use the excess to pay off credit card debt, as well as other personal expenses. Of that amount, $300,000 (the replacement of your outstanding balance) is treated as deductible acquisition debt, while $100,000 is treated as deductible home equity debt, but interest on the remaining $50,000 is nondeductible.

FAILING TO SECURE...

A loan not secured by a residence does not produce deductible mortgage interest.

EXAMPLE: Parents lend a child $20,000 to make a down payment on a house. Even though the money is used to buy the home, the child cannot deduct mortgage interest on the loan unless it is secured by the home just as the primary mortgage is.

INVESTMENT BORROWING...

Deduction rules for investment borrowing are the *opposite* of those for home-equity borrowing—the loan need not be secured by an investment, but it must be spent on an investment—except for tax-exempt securities.

If a parent lends funds to a child who uses them to make investments, the child can deduct interest paid to the parent on the loan under normal investment interest rules.

IMPORTANT: Intrafamily loans must have reasonable terms, be documented and the terms must be followed—or you risk having the IRS treat them as gifts.

BUSINESS BORROWING...

Interest on this is deductible without limit if borrowed funds are used for legitimate business purposes. An undocumented loan, or one whose terms are not followed, may be deemed by the IRS to be an equity investment—disallowing all interest.

NOTE: Borrowing money to buy stock in a business is treated as investment borrowing and the deduction is subject to the investment interest limitations mentioned previously.

■

REPORT #36

THE IRS IS WATCHING!

Source: IRS Press Release.

Credit card companies are helping the IRS catch tax evaders by providing information about customers who have offshore accounts. In 2002, MasterCard turned over information on 230,000 accounts and American Express also agreed to provide similar information.

All of this is part of an IRS program to identify persons who open foreign bank accounts to avoid paying tax on income earned in them.

■

REPORT #37

PAY ZERO TAX WHEN SELLING YOUR HOME

Source: **C. Anthony Phillips, CPA,** president of Downstream Exchange Company, an accommodator of tax-deferred exchanges, in Pasadena, CA. He is a frequent speaker at conferences of the Federation of Exchange Accommodators and a faculty member of the California Association of Realtors.

In today's marketplace of skyrocketing house prices, the home sale capital gain exclusion may not help you much. This tax exclusion is limited to $250,000 for taxpayers filing singly and $500,000 for married couples filing jointly. But what happens if your home has appreciated in value by far more than the exclusion amount?

LOOPHOLE: There is a way to extract cash from highly appreciated residential property while avoiding the tax that you would pay if you sold it outright. **HERE ARE THE DETAILS...**

SWAP RATHER THAN SELL...

You can defer tax on a home's appreciation by using the like-kind exchange rules that are found in Section 1031 of the Tax Code. These rules allow business or investment property to be traded tax free for another business or investment property. Any potential gain is deferred until the replacement property (the property acquired in the exchange) is subsequently sold.

REQUIREMENT: For the exchange of a principal residence to qualify, it's necessary to convert the home to business or investment property.

REFINANCE AND SWAP: Let's say a single home owner purchased a home for $200,000 that is now worth $2 million—so there's a potential gain of $1.8 million. The home owner can refinance the mortgage to pull out cash, up to the equity in the home. Typically, mortgages are offered on up to 80% of the value of a home after factoring in repayment of any outstanding mortgage. Assuming this home owner has no mortgage, he/she obtains $1.6 million cash (80% of the $2 million value) by taking a mortgage on the home. Some or all of the money is then used to purchase a new home.

Then he rents out the old home, thus converting it to investment property. After a time—typically a year or two to establish the home as an investment property—when the home is worth, say, $2.2 million, he "exchanges" (details below) the now rental property for another like-kind property. This could be a strip mall, office building, other rental housing or any other investment property worth at least $2.2 million. The like-kind requirements are met because he's exchanging his rental real property for rental real property.

RESULT: The home owner pockets no cash (remember that at least a $1.6 million mortgage needs to be obtained on the replacement property, and the remaining cash must be used to acquire the replacement property when the home is exchanged) and owns rental property worth $2.2 million or more. And, there are no current taxes on the deal!

IRS BLESSING...

Can you use both the home sale exclusion and Section 1031? The IRS has recently issued guidance on this point, allowing a home owner to benefit from both the home sale exclusion and the like-kind exchange rules [Revenue Procedure 2005-14].

Under this guidance, a home owner may be able to use the exclusion *and* the exchange rules to avoid all current tax on an exchange, while increasing the basis of replacement property.

KEY: The home owner must have owned and lived in the home for at least two of the five years before the date of the exchange. This is required for the home sale exclusion.

Say he lived in the home from 1990 to 2004, and then rented out the place in 2005 and 2006. The home qualifies for the exclusion because the home owner met the two-out-of-five-year requirement and, since it has been converted to rental property, for like-kind exchange treatment as well.

In this example, the IRS views the first $250,000 ($500,000 if married) of the $2 million gain as qualifying for the home sale exclusion (the exclusion must be applied first). The balance of the gain ($1.75 million) is then tax deferred under the like-kind exchange rule.

EVEN BETTER: The home can be depreciated throughout the rental period, yet there will be no depreciation recapture required upon its exchange. Recapture is required only when there is a recognized gain. Since the property is exchanged, no gain is recognized.

If the home owner had received cash as part of the exchange —to account for a difference in the value between the exchanged properties—then the gain would have been taxable to the extent of this "boot." Depreciation recapture may affect the tax rate paid on this amount—in this example, it would be 25% instead of the 15% capital gains rate.

NEWLY ACQUIRED PROPERTY...

What is the basis in the property acquired in exchange for the old residence? This is important to know for purposes of figuring depreciation on the replacement property.

According to the IRS guidance, the basis of the replacement property is the basis of the relinquished property, increased by the exclusion amount. In effect, the home sale exclusion amount is treated as gain on the exchange, which serves to increase the basis of the replacement property.

Recall that in the example above, the basis of the original home was $200,000. Therefore, the basis of the replacement property will be $450,000 (that's $200,000, increased by the excluded gain of $250,000).

THE NITTY-GRITTY...

• *Rules for like-kind exchanges.* It is often difficult for a tax-payer to swap an investment property for another investment property. Additional strict timing rules can make effecting an exchange even more difficult. For these reasons, it may be prudent to use an *accommodator,* a person who helps complete a deferred exchange. In addition to preparing documents to facilitate an exchange and holding on to the proceeds from escrow, an accommodator, if qualified, will give tax advice on various aspects of the exchange.

HOW THE PROCESS WORKS: First, the taxpayer enters into an escrow for the sale of their investment property. Then the accommodator advises the taxpayer about the requirements to successfully complete an exchange and the tax law's time limits. (After the close of escrow, the taxpayer has 45 days in which to identify properties that may be the target of an exchange. The taxpayer identifies the property in a signed statement delivered to the accommodator. The taxpayer then has 180 days from the close of escrow in which to close on the acquisition of the targeted property.)

CAUTION: These time limits are very strict. They are not extended even when a deadline day falls on a Saturday, Sunday or holiday. It is the accommodator's job to see that these limits are understood and satisfied.

NOTE: The taxpayer, and not the accommodator, is responsible for finding the replacement property, which may be done through a real estate agent.

• *Home sale exclusion rules.* If the taxpayer receives a rental residence in an exchange and then subsequently converts it to his principal residence, another home sale exclusion cannot be taken on a future sale of this residence unless a "special use" test is satisfied. Instead of the usual two-year use requirement, a taxpayer who acquires a residence in a like-kind exchange must live in the home for at least two years and own it for five years prior to a future sale to qualify for the exclusion.

■

REPORT #38

HANDS OFF MY MONEY, IRS!

Source: **Michael E. Mares, Esq., CPA/ABV**, tax member, Witt, Mares & Company, PLC, 701 Town Center Dr., Newport News, VA 23606. He is coauthor of *Guide to Limited Liability Companies* (Practitioners Publishing).

The next best thing to tax-free income is *tax-deferred* income. A concept called the *time value of money* comes into play when tax is deferred—a dollar today is worth more than a dollar tomorrow because of its earnings potential in the interim.

HERE ARE 15 WAYS YOU CAN DEFER TAXES TO INCREASE YOUR WEALTH...

RETIREMENT PLANNING...

1. *Deferred compensation.* Some companies offer employees the option of deferring the receipt of some of their earnings, such as year-end bonuses, to a future date. But, since the income has been earned already, tax on it can be deferred only if certain requirements are met (e.g., the agreement to defer income must have been made at the start of the year in which it is earned).

The deferred compensation is subject to FICA (Social Security and Medicare) taxes in the year it is earned, not in the year it is paid out to you. If your income in the year you earn the money exceeds the Social Security wage base ($94,200 in 2006), the deferred compensation will never be subjected to Social Security tax.

2. *Individual retirement accounts (IRAs).* Traditional IRAs let you receive a deduction now for contributions that will grow unimpeded by taxes until distributions are taken.

Deferral must begin phasing out, however, when the owner turns age 70½. At this time, distributions must be taken according to required minimum distribution rules, which are essentially designed to draw down the account over the owner's lifetime.

EXTRA DEFERRAL: The IRA owner can postpone the first required minimum distribution to April 1 of the year following the year in which he/she turns age 70½. However, doing this means taking the second required minimum distribution in the same year (by December 31).

3. *Employer retirement plans.* Employees and self-employed individuals who participate in company plans, which can include 401(k)s, 403(b) annuities, simplified employee pension (SEP) plans and Savings Incentive Match Plans for Employees of Small Employers (SIMPLEs), achieve tax deferral for investments in their accounts. Contributions build up on a tax-deferred basis. As with IRAs, deferral continues until the year in which you turn age 70½ (or the following April 1). At that time, required minimum distributions must begin.

ADDITIONAL DEFERRAL: If you are still working at this age and your plan allows it, you can postpone distributions until the end of the year in which you actually retire, giving you more years of tax-deferred earnings.

HEALTH/EDUCATION SAVINGS...

4. *Health savings accounts (HSAs).* When you are covered by a high-deductible health plan, you—or your employer on your behalf—can make tax-deductible contributions to an HSA, a savings account for medical costs. Funds accrue tax deferred.

Withdrawals for medical expenses not covered by insurance are tax free. Withdrawals for nonmedical purposes can be made but are taxable.

TRAP: If you are under age 65 when you take nonmedical distributions, withdrawals are also subject to a 10% penalty.

5. *Section 529 plans.* Saving for higher-education costs for your child or grandchild can be done through savings plans and prepaid tuition plans, collectively called 529 plans (after the Tax Code section governing them). Contributions are not deductible, but earnings on them build up on a tax-deferred basis. Distributions to pay qualified educational expenses, such as tuition and fees, books, supplies and equipment required for enrollment or attendance are tax free.

IMPORTANT: There's no age limit on how long funds can remain in the plan—deferral can go on until the beneficiary dies, at which point remaining funds are included in his estate.

6. *Coverdell Education Savings Accounts (ESAs).* As with 529 accounts, contributions go into these accounts on an after-tax basis, then funds accumulate tax-deferred and can be taken out to pay a wide range of education costs from kindergarten through college and graduate school.

CAUTION: The earnings portion of distributions taken for noneducation purposes is taxable, plus there is a 10% penalty on such withdrawals.

If funds remain in the account when the beneficiary reaches age 30, they become taxable. But deferral can be continued by naming a new (younger) beneficiary who is a member of the original beneficiary's family (spouse, child, grandchild, sibling, etc.).

INVESTMENT OPPORTUNITIES...

7. *Six-month CDs and Treasury bills.* Financial instruments with six-month maturities acquired after June 30 of a given year allow you to defer tax on interest earned in the year of purchase to the following year. Now that short-term interest rates have been rising, such investments may look particularly attractive.

8. Savings bonds. Series EE, I and E savings bonds issued after December 1965 all have a 30-year maturity. Interest accrues on these bonds on a tax-deferred basis.

Interest on bonds purchased after 1989 by a person at least age 24 can become tax free if the bonds are redeemed to pay for qualified educational expenses and one's modified adjusted gross income doesn't exceed the limit ($63,100 single, $94,700 joint). There is an income phaseout (up to $78,100 single or $124,700 joint) in which interest may be partially tax free.

9. Commercial annuities. Earnings on money that is invested in commercial (as opposed to private or employee) annuities, other than immediate annuities that start payments at once, build up on a tax-deferred basis. When annuity payments are received, only the portion that's related to earnings becomes taxable—the balance is a tax-free return of your investment. The payouts are partially taxable based upon the expected return compared with the amount paid for the annuity.

10. Installment sales. If you sell property for a gain and receive one or more payments after the year of sale, you report your gain only when and to the extent that payments are received. Tax is deferred until then.

CHOICE: You can opt to report all of the gain in the year of sale, depending on your particular tax situation, simply by entering it on Schedule D (for capital assets) or Form 4797, *Sales of Business Property.*

11. Like-kind exchanges. When you swap a property that is "similar or related in service or use," such as one rental property for another, you can postpone reporting gain on the original property until you dispose of the replacement property.

NOTE: A precise sequence of events has to happen to be eligible. See IRS Publication 544, *Sales and Other Dispositions of Assets.*

12. Involuntary conversions. When a property is damaged by storm or some similar event, insurance proceeds can exceed the property basis, which is considered a gain. But reporting the gain for tax purposes can be postponed in a manner similar to a like-kind exchange. You must invest your gain in suitable replacement property within two years of the end of the year of the gain (four years for a personal residence, five years for Katrina-damaged property). See IRS Publication 547, *Casualties, Disasters, and Thefts;* Publication 2194, *2005 Disaster Losses Kit for Individuals;* and Publication 2194B, *2005 Disaster Losses Kit for Businesses.*

13. *Condemnation.* If real property you own is seized by eminent domain and the proceeds from the state or municipality exceed your basis, gain can be postponed by acquiring replacement property within three years for business or investment real estate or two years for a principal residence.

14. *Selling short.* When you make a short sale of an investment security, gain is not reported until you close the sale by delivering replacement stock to the broker.

CAUTION: Holding an appreciated position in the same stock ("selling short against the box") is treated as a constructive sale of the appreciated position, requiring income reporting in that year even if replacement stock is not delivered until the next year.

15. *Master limited partnerships (MLPs).* Because of the partnership structure and special tax rules for MLPs, the bulk of annual distributions to limited partners (investors) is shielded from current tax—the deferral percentage will typically range from 75% to 90%, although the percentage can decline over the years. When the units are sold, tax becomes due on the amount shielded.

■

REPORT #39

THE BUSINESS TRAVEL LOOPHOLE THE IRS DOESN'T WANT YOU TO KNOW

Source: **Bernard S. Kent, Esq., CPA,** human resource services partner, PricewaterhouseCoopers LLP, 400 Renaissance Center, Detroit 48243. He is past chairman of the personal financial planning committee of the Michigan Association of Certified Public Accountants and coauthor of *PricewaterhouseCoopers Guide to Tax and Financial Planning, 2007: How the 2006 Tax Law Changes Affect You* (Wiley).

If you're self-employed or run your own company, you have considerable leeway in setting your business travel plans.

With some forethought—and a great deal of diligent record keeping—you can legitimately convert leisure travel costs into tax-deductible business expenses.

DOMESTIC TRIPS...

Travel within the United States is deductible if the trip is primarily for business.

INCLUDED: Airfare, airport parking, cabs, car rentals, tips.

What makes a trip primarily for business? If you go to Milwaukee to see clients for a week and spend an afternoon playing golf, that's a business trip. The line can be blurred if you mix less business with more pleasure—say, go to San Francisco for a business meal or two, then tour the wine country for the weekend.

STRATEGY: Make sure that the majority of the days involved are business days. For example, if you're away for a week, include at least four business days. The IRS generally accepts a broad definition of business days (that is, days during which you materially conduct business). You don't need to devote the entire day to business for it to count.

EXAMPLES: Days traveling to and from a business trip are business days, as well as weekends and holidays in between weekday business meetings. That's especially true if staying over saves you money.

SATURDAY NIGHT SPECIAL: Say you have business meetings in Chicago, Monday through Friday, and based on available flights, going home on Sunday gives you a much lower airfare than going home Friday night or Saturday.

RESULT: You book a return flight on Sunday. Saturday and Sunday count as business days when determining whether your airfare is deductible.

The same is true if you have business meetings Friday and the following Monday—you stay the weekend to avoid paying for travel back and forth, so the weekend counts as business days.

COMBINATION PLAYS...

With those ground rules in mind, you can see how to combine business and leisure travel.

EXAMPLE: You're going to New York City for an industry convention, which will require a total of five business days, including travel.

If you add an extra three or four days to your trip for personal pursuits, the trip still counts as a business trip because the majority of days are used for business, so your travel costs will be fully tax deductible.

PUTTING PLEASURE FIRST: Another approach is to decide when and where you would like to vacation, then construct a business trip around that plan by arranging business meetings in that area before you go. As long as more than half of the days can be counted as business days, you can deduct your travel costs.

ROOM AND BOARD...

In today's world, with frequent-flier miles and steep airline discounts, transportation outlays may be a minor portion of your overall trip costs.

SIGNIFICANT NONTRAVEL EXPENSES: Especially if your business is conducted in major metropolitan areas, hotel and meal costs can easily outstrip airfares. Therefore, the ability to deduct those costs can be very valuable. **WHAT'S DEDUCTIBLE...**

• *Hotels.* You can deduct the hotel costs incurred for business days—the nights before and after doing business, for instance, and weekend stays that cut travel costs.

And, if you take a day off during a week of business meetings, you're unlikely to face a challenge if you deduct all of your hotel bill.

CAUTION: If you take a business trip and arrive several days early or stay late, just for a vacation, you cannot deduct the hotel costs for these nonbusiness days.

Therefore, you might be better off truly mixing your business and pleasure days. Do business at the beginning and the end of your trip. You can make a strong case for deducting hotel days that are bookended by business days.

• *Meals and entertainment.* The Tax Code limits these deductions, as they relate to business meetings and other business contacts, to 50%. So, for every $100 you spend taking contacts to dinner or to basketball games, only $50 can be deducted.

Meals you eat by yourself are 50% deductible as well, as long as you eat those meals while away on business.

TRAVEL COMPANIONS...

You may want to take your spouse or other companion (and perhaps your children) with you on business trips.

REQUIRED: For a companion's travel costs to be deductible, he/she must be an employee on your company's payroll, going along for a genuine business purpose.

If those conditions aren't met, though, you probably can still deduct business-related hotel costs, even if you share the room. In addition, you can take a 50% deduction if you pick up the check for a business meal where spouses are present.

FOREIGN TRAVEL...

The rules are a bit different if you leave the US on business.

IF YOUR FOREIGN TRIP LASTS...

• *Seven days or less,* including one travel day, four business days will make it a business trip—the same as within the US. Your travel expenses are deductible.

• *More than seven days,* then you need to calculate how much time you spend on nonbusiness activities. If you spend at least 25% of the days that you're away from home vacationing, the trip isn't considered a pure business trip. If you do some real business on any one given day, you have reason to designate it as a business day.

RESULT: For a week-plus, business/pleasure trip, you need to make an allocation between work and play.

EXAMPLE: You go to England for a total of 10 days, including three days that involve nothing but sightseeing. You can deduct only 70% of your travel costs.

STRATEGY: If possible, keep foreign business trips within the seven-day limit, so your tax write-off will extend to your leisure time, too.

RELY ON RECORDS...

As mentioned, arranging appointments in advance can help you mix in some vacation time with tax-deductible travel, foreign or domestic.

KEY: If it's practical, try to minimize days spent entirely on pleasurable pursuits.

A genuine business meeting or attendance at a convention session will make that day a tax-deductible business day, even if you take some time off to play tennis or have a purely social restaurant meal.

STRATEGY: Make sure to keep thorough records, including phone logs and e-mail correspondence involved in setting up meetings. If you go to a convention, keep a copy of the program and any notes you took during the session.

After your return, send letters or e-mail to the people you met, referring to the business purpose of your encounter. Keep copies, along with any evidence that your business was enhanced by the encounter.

BOTTOM LINE: Never hesitate to deduct your legitimate travel and entertainment costs when you prepare your tax return. However, claimed travel and entertainment deductions may attract the attention of IRS agents, so be prepared to justify any deduction.

The more paperwork you have showing the business purpose of your travel, the more likely your deductions will be sustained.

■

REPORT #40

BEAT THE TAX MAN LEGALLY

Source: **Bernard S. Kent, Esq., CPA,** human resource services partner, PricewaterhouseCoopers LLP, 400 Renaissance Center, Detroit 48243. He is past chairman of the personal financial planning committee of the Michigan Association of Certified Public Accountants and coauthor of *PricewaterhouseCoopers Guide to Tax and Financial Planning, 2007: How the 2006 Tax Law Changes Affect You* (Wiley).

When you retire, the paychecks stop but the taxes don't. Your income may be fixed, or nearly so, if you rely on Social Security, a pension, an annuity, etc. Meanwhile, taxes can eat up more and more of the money you need for living.

Here are ways to fight the tax hit...

PROPERTY TAXES...

For many people on modest incomes, property taxes can be higher than income taxes. **TAKE THESE STEPS...**

• *Apply for a senior property tax break.* Many states offer such programs. There may be income or other limitations. Contact your state's revenue (tax) department to find out what's available and how to apply.

EXAMPLE: Some Illinois seniors can cut their property taxes by as much as $3,000 per year, thanks to a "senior citizen's homestead exemption."

RESOURCE: Federation of Tax Administrators (*www.taxad min.org/fta/link*) has links to every state's tax authority.

• *Appeal your property assessment if you think you pay much higher taxes than your neighbors for a similar house.* If successful, you may be able to reduce your annual tax bill.

HOW TO DO IT: Contact your town or county assessor's office to get the information on which it based your assessment. Look for outright mistakes about your property, such as the wrong square footage, number of bedrooms or lot size. There also may be external factors that reduce the property's value, such as heavy traffic and/or noise near your house.

DEADLINE ALERT: Each jurisdiction has an "appeal season," generally several months early in the year. Contact your jurisdiction to determine your window of opportunity.

You may be able simply to show your evidence to the county assessor to have your assessment reduced. If informal procedures don't work, go before the local assessment board to make your case.

• *Sell your house.* As long as you have owned and occupied the house for at least two of the last five years, you'll owe no tax on up to $250,000 worth of profit from the sale ($500,000 for married couples). You then can move into an apartment or buy a house with lower taxes.

If you would like to remain in your house, you can sell it to a grown son or daughter and pay him/her rent to live there. You'll pocket your tax-free gain, and, as long as you pay a fair market rent, the new owner will be entitled to the tax benefits of owning rental property—such as deductions for depreciation.

FEDERAL INCOME TAXES...

If your taxable income is below $50,000 and your finances are relatively straightforward, it might pay for you to take the standard deduction on IRS Form 1040EZ or Form 1040A for your federal tax return. These forms are short and simple. Otherwise, using these forms might lock you out of certain deductions and/or credits and cause you to overpay your taxes.

EXAMPLE: If your unreimbursed medical expenses total more than 7.5% of your adjusted gross income, you can itemize and deduct them—but only on Form 1040, the regular "long" form.

To further cut your taxes...

• **Use borrowing power.** The IRS taxes *income.* Money that you *borrow* can provide cash flow without raising your tax bill. Use borrowed money, tax-free, for some of your expenses. Today's low interest rates make such an approach practical.

EXAMPLES: You might use a home-equity line of credit with a very favorable interest rate. The interest you pay probably will be deductible if you itemize on Form 1040.

For information on home-equity interest deductibility, see IRS publication 936, *Home Mortgage Interest Deduction,* available from the IRS at 800-TAX-FORM or *www.irs.gov.*

Another possibility is to take out a loan against your cash-value life insurance or your securities portfolio.

STRATEGY: Keep the bulk of your long-term noncash savings in assets that do not generate much taxable income, such as growth stocks or tax-managed mutual funds.

WARNING: Don't borrow at high interest rates or to excess. You might endanger your core assets—your investment portfolio, insurance policies, even your house.

• **Let your house pay you.** If you are at least 62 years old and your home is not heavily mortgaged, consider taking out a reverse mortgage. You'll get tax-free cash, and the money doesn't have to be repaid until you die or move out of the house.

INFORMATION: AARP, 888-687-2277, *www.aarp.org/revmort.*

STATE AND LOCAL INCOME TAXES...

Some state and local governments provide seniors with income tax breaks that shelter pension and/or Social Security benefits. For information, contact your tax adviser or state tax authority.

EXAMPLE: Michigan offers married couples an income tax exclusion for up to $77,100 of annual private (nongovernment) pension income. Single filers can exclude up to $38,550.

If your income is high and/or you live in an area that has high taxes even for seniors, you might want to move to a less taxing jurisdiction. Before you pick a new place to live, be sure to take all of its taxes into account. A state might have low income tax, but the area you like might have high property tax. For help comparing overall tax burdens in various states, call the Tax Foundation at 202-464-6200 or visit *www.taxfoundation.org.*

CAUTION: States chase down residents who try to illegally avoid taxes by claiming they've moved, perhaps by buying or renting a second home or even using a relative's address.

If you move, be sure to sever your connections to your old state. Move your bank accounts, turn in your driver's license after you get one from your new state, register to vote in your new jurisdiction, etc.

File a final income tax return with your former state, and subsequently file returns with your new state if required. Use your new address on all tax documents, and file federal returns with the IRS Service Center for your new state.

■

HEALTH

5

HEALTH

REPORT #41

ERASE YOUR HOT FLASHES FAST!

Source: **Gregory L. Burke, MD,** professor and vice chair, department of public health services, Bowman Gray School of Medicine, Winston–Salem, NC.

Try eating more soy. In a study, menopausal women who added 20 grams of soy powder per day (about four tablespoons) to their diets reported reduced severity of hot flashes and night sweats.

BONUS: Their cholesterol levels also fell.

THEORY: Soy contains *isoflavones*, which are compounds that mimic the beneficial effects of estrogen with less risks. Estrogen-replacement therapy raises the risk of breast and ovarian cancer.

Soy powder, available at health food stores, can be added to juice, cereals and other foods.

■

REPORT #42

THE LITTLE PILL THAT WILL SAVE YOUR LIFE

The group of drugs called *statins* lowers LDL ("bad") cholesterol and reduces the risk of heart attack by as much as 50% and stroke by 25%—but that's not all. Recent research suggests that statins have other remarkable health benefits, too.

The statins, which include *atorvastatin* (Lipitor), *pravastatin* (Pravachol), *simvastatin* (Zocor) and others, limit the amount of cholesterol that is produced in the liver. They also have powerful anti-inflammatory and antioxidant effects that prevent cell and tissue damage. The majority of patients who take them experience few or no side effects, although the drugs can be dangerous for some people.

More studies are needed before doctors can recommend taking statins solely for Alzheimer's, cancer and eye diseases, but people with rheumatoid arthritis or diabetes should ask about statin therapy.

Several prominent medical experts have found statins to be particularly effective in preventing and treating the following diseases. HERE'S WHAT THEY FOUND...

ALZHEIMER'S DISEASE...

Large observational studies suggest that people who take statins may reduce their risk of getting Alzheimer's by 30% to 70%. Statins also may delay the onset of Alzheimer's symptoms.

HOW THEY WORK: Statins appear to protect the brain in ways unrelated to their cholesterol-lowering effects. Patients who have Alzheimer's disease accumulate higher-than-normal levels of amyloid proteins, which form gumlike insoluble plaque in the brain. The immune system detects this plaque and releases inflammatory molecules in an attempt to destroy it. Persistent inflammation damages surrounding brain cells without breaking down the plaque. Statins may reduce brain damage by controlling this inflammatory process.

Source: **Majid Fotuhi, MD, PhD,** assistant professor of neurology at Johns Hopkins University School of Medicine and director of the Memory Disorders Unit at Sinai Hospital of Baltimore. He is author of *The Memory Cure: How to Protect Your Brain Against Memory Loss and Alzheimer's Disease* (McGraw-Hill).

CANCER...

Statins may help prevent cancer. An Israeli study of 3,342 patients found that those taking statins were about 50% less likely to get colon cancer. Other studies indicate that statins can reduce the risk of prostate cancer by up to 56% and risk of breast cancer by 30%.

HOW THEY WORK: Statins may block the activation of an enzyme complex (*proteasome*) that breaks down proteins. Inhibiting this process may cause cancer cells to die rather than proliferate. It is also possible that statins block cell signals that can trigger cancerous cell division.

In addition, changes in cholesterol metabolism in those taking statins may result in less free testosterone in the blood, which may reduce prostate cancer risk.

Source: **Sheldon Marks, MD,** associate clinical professor of urology and clinical lecturer in radiation oncology at the University of Arizona College of Medicine, Tucson, and adjunct assistant professor of urology at Tufts University School of Medicine, Boston. He is author of *Prostate and Cancer* (Perseus) and directs the men's health message board at WebMD.com.

EYE DISEASES...

Long-term use of statins may protect vision. They can reduce the risk of glaucoma, which causes a loss of peripheral vision and sometimes results in blindness. Damage to the optic nerve usually is accompanied by abnormally high pressure inside the eyeball.

Researchers at the University of Alabama at Birmingham examined the medical records of 667 men over age 50 who had been diagnosed with glaucoma and compared them with the records of men without glaucoma. The men who had taken statins for two years or more were 40% less likely to develop glaucoma.

Other studies suggest that statins may reduce the risk of developing age-related macular degeneration, the leading cause of blindness in people age 65 and older.

HOW THEY WORK: Statins improve circulation, which brings healing nutrients to the eyes while promoting drainage that reduces pressure buildup.

CAUTION: Eye specialists have seen a slight increase in cataracts in patients using statins. Anyone taking these drugs should have regular eye exams.

Source: **Robert Abel, Jr., MD,** ophthalmologist in private practice in Wilmington, DE, and former clinical professor of ophthalmology at Thomas Jefferson University, Philadelphia. He is author of *The Eye Care Revolution* (Kensington).

RHEUMATOID ARTHRITIS...

Statins may reduce pain and minimize joint damage.

HOW THEY WORK: Statins reduce inflammation, an underlying cause of rheumatoid arthritis. Researchers in Glasgow, Scotland, gave either Lipitor or a placebo to 116 patients with rheumatoid arthritis. After six months, patients taking Lipitor had fewer swollen joints and lower levels of *C-reactive protein* and other markers of inflammation.

IMPORTANT: Consider statin therapy in addition to traditional therapy—even if you don't have high cholesterol—if you have risk factors for heart problems, such as a family history of heart disease. A recent study found that women who had rheumatoid arthritis for at least 10 years were three times more likely to have a heart attack than women who didn't have the condition.

Source: **David Borenstein, MD,** clinical professor of medicine at George Washington University Medical Center and in private practice at Arthritis and Rheumatism Associates, both in Washington, DC. He is author of *Back in Control* (Evans and Co.).

DIABETES...

Most diabetes patients should consider taking a statin drug, according to the latest American Diabetes Association guidelines. The updated guidelines reflect the results of the Heart Protection Study, which found that people with diabetes could reduce their risk of having a heart attack or stroke with statins even if their cholesterol levels were normal. The guidelines recommend statins for people over age 40 who have diabetes and who have total cholesterol of 135 or higher.

Source: **Boris Draznin, MD, PhD,** professor of medicine at the University of Colorado School of Medicine, Denver, and associate chief of staff of research and development at the Denver Veterans Affairs Medical Center. He is author of *The Thinking Person's Guide to Diabetes: The Draznin Plan* (Oxford).

REPORT #43

THE HIGH BLOOD PRESSURE BREAKTHROUGH

Source: **Alexa Fleckenstein, MD,** board-certified internist who practices traditional and complementary medicine, Boston. Dr. Fleckenstein holds a German subspecialty degree in natural medicine.

For most Americans, a steaming hot bath or shower is a daily routine. But for more than 150 years, numerous Europeans have used invigorating *cold* showers and swims to promote good health.

Scientific evidence and numerous case histories support the use of "cold-water therapy" as an adjunct to standard treatments for frequent colds, insomnia, high blood pressure—even cancer and other serious disorders.

HOW IT BEGAN...

Cold-water therapy was first popularized in Germany by the priest Sebastian Kneipp (1821–1897). In the winter of 1849, Kneipp successfully battled then-incurable tuberculosis by plunging several times weekly into the frigid Danube River. His 1886 book, *My Water Cure*, became an international best-seller.

THE MECHANISM...

When practiced for at least four weeks, cold-water therapy...

• *Stabilizes blood pressure.* Cold water triggers the autonomic nervous system—which controls involuntary functions, such as heartbeat and breathing—to raise blood pressure, increase heart rate and constrict blood vessels.

The autonomic responses strengthen with each exposure. This stabilizes blood pressure, improves circulation and balances other bodily functions, such as the sleep/wake cycle.

• *Enhances immunity.* Cold water triggers the release of cytokines and other hormone-like substances that are key to improving immune function.

RECENT FINDING: Breast cancer patients who underwent four weeks of cold-water therapy experienced significant gains in their levels of disease-fighting white blood cells, according to a German study.

• *Reduces pain.* Cold causes the body to release *endorphins,* hormones with proven pain-fighting properties.

• *Improves moods.* Cold water activates sensory nerves that lead to the brain. A cold, exhilarating shower can be emotionally uplifting and prime a person for new experiences.

THE REGIMEN...

To gain the benefits of cold-water therapy at home, begin with your usual warm shower. When you're finished, step out of the water stream and turn off the hot water. Leave the cold water running.*

Start by wetting your feet first. Next, expose your hands and face to the cold water.

IMPORTANT: Jumping in all at once may hinder circulation.

Finally, step under the shower. Let the cold water run over your scalp, face, the front of your body and then down your back. You can begin by taking a cold shower that lasts only a couple of seconds.

After a month, the entire process should last no more than 40 seconds. Work up to whatever is comfortable for you.

IF YOU CAN'T TOLERATE THE COLD: Keep the water cold but expose only your feet, hands and face. Gradually increase the duration and area of exposure.

CAUTION: People who are very thin or frail may be unable to tolerate cold showers in the beginning. If you do not feel warm and invigorated after the shower, decrease the length of your next cold shower.

If you still don't feel warm within minutes, forgo cold showers. Instead, condition your body with cold sponge baths of the feet, hands, face—and then the rest of your body—after your warm shower.

Do not try cold-water therapy if you suffer from an acute illness, such as severe back pain...have hardening of the arteries (atherosclerosis)...Raynaud's disease...or have high blood pressure not controlled by medication.

*Water temperature should be about 60°F. In all but the hottest areas, water straight from the cold faucet will do. If your water is not cold enough to give you a good jolt, enhance the effect by air-drying—rather than towel drying—your body.

Cold water causes a spike in blood pressure, which can be dangerous for those who have conditions such as unmanaged hypertension.

The therapy can be safely used to reduce mildly elevated blood pressure (150/100 and below) or to raise low blood pressure.

IF YOU HAVE QUESTIONS ABOUT YOUR BLOOD PRESSURE: See your doctor for a blood pressure test before starting a cold-water regimen.

■

REPORT #44

CANCER-FREE FOR LIFE

Source: **Melanie Polk, RD,** director, nutrition education, American Institute for Cancer Research, 1759 R St. NW, Washington, DC 20009, *www.aicr.org.*

People often assume that cancer is out of their hands because it is "genetic." In fact, lifestyle decisions are much more important in determining who gets cancer—and who does not.

Even if your genes place you at risk for cancer, 60% to 70% of all malignancies can be avoided by paying attention to four lifestyle factors—diet, weight control, exercise and not smoking.

IF YOU MAKE JUST ONE CHANGE...

Eating a plant-based diet is the single most important thing you can do to help lower your cancer risk.

Foods should be minimally processed and eaten as close to their natural state as possible. Processed foods may have lost some of their nutritional value.

EXAMPLE: Eat a potato rather than chips or french fries.

Also limit intake of foods with added sugar, such as soft drinks and sweetened cereals.

If you eat red meat regularly, try to have no more than three ounces per day.

Eating at least five servings—about one-half cup each—of fruits or vegetables every day can decrease your risk of developing cancer by 20%.

OTHER IMPORTANT STEPS...

• *Maintain a healthful weight,* and be physically active. Try not to gain too much weight after reaching your full height (at about age 18 for women...24 for men).

Start by walking every day—working your way up to a brisk, one-hour walk daily. In addition, work up a sweat by engaging in some form of vigorous physical activity for at least one hour each week.

• *Drink alcohol in moderation*—if at all. There is no evidence that alcohol reduces cancer risk, though some evidence suggests that moderate alcohol consumption helps prevent coronary artery disease in men and possibly women. If you do drink, limit your consumption to one drink a day for women... two drinks a day for men.

Avoid alcohol entirely if you are a woman who has an increased risk for breast cancer.

• *Select foods that are low in fat and salt.* Limit your intake of fatty foods. Use a moderate amount of monounsaturated oils, such as olive and canola.

Avoid animal fat and hydrogenated fat, which is commonly found in shortening, margarine and bakery items.

Watch those snack foods, salty condiments and pickles.

• *Prepare and store foods safely.* Keep cold foods cold and hot foods hot.

If you eat meat, avoid charring it. Limit your intake of cured or smoked meat. Take precautions when grilling—trim the fat from meat, marinate it, then microwave it for half the cooking time before grilling.

• *Avoid tobacco in any form.*

CANCER RISK FACTORS...

Anticancer precautions are particularly important for individuals at increased risk for cancer. THESE RISK FACTORS INCLUDE...*

• *Family history of genetically linked types of cancer,* such as breast, ovarian and colon cancers.

• *Inflammatory bowel disease.*

• *Human papillomavirus (HPV) infection.*

*This information is based on a major study by the American Institute for Cancer Research that reviewed more than 4,500 studies to determine the relationships among diet, lifestyle and cancer risk.

- *Alcoholism.*
- *Hepatitis B or C virus (HBV/HCV).*
Additional risk factors for women...
- *First menstrual period before the age of 12.*
- *First child born after age 30.*
- *Childless and over age 50.*
- *Postmenopausal and on hormone-replacement therapy.*

■

REPORT #45

THE HIGH-SPEED, HOLLYWOOD SHAPE-UP PLAN

Source: **Greg Isaacs,** celebrity trainer and former director, corporate fitness, Warner Bros. Studios, Burbank, CA. He is author of *The Ultimate Lean Routine* (Summit).

As a trainer who works with professional actors and actresses—who are some of the most body-conscious people in the world—I have found that they aren't very different from you and me.

Like average people, many actors eat out of emotion...have sedentary jobs...often dislike exercising...have erratic work schedules...and are frequently in situations where tempting, high-calorie foods are offered.

What makes them different is that their jobs depend on being fit and trim. That gives them a very special incentive to get in shape and stay that way.

You don't have to be a celebrity to have a body like one. You just have to be willing to work out like one. I recommend the following exercises to all of my clients.

IMPORTANT: For each exercise, do three sets of eight to 12 repetitions. Perform each of the exercises slowly. You'll strengthen your muscles faster and with fewer repetitions this way. Increase the weight of your dumbbells as soon as an exercise becomes easy for you to perform.

SCULPTED ARMS AND SHOULDERS...

Do push-ups. Position yourself on all fours on the floor. Keep your upper body and your elbows straight and place your hands beneath your shoulders.

Either bend your legs at the knees and cross your ankles—the easiest way to do push-ups—or keep your legs straight and balance on your toes for the greatest benefit.

Lower your chest to the floor using only your arms. Then raise your chest off the floor using only your arms until your elbows are straight again—but not locked. Repeat.

BULGING BICEPS...

Do a biceps curl using an eight- to 10-pound weight. Stand or sit. Stick your chin up and your chest out. Keep your elbows in—close to your sides—palms forward. Don't cheat by letting your elbow swing back and forth as you lift the weight or by leaning forward to begin a lift. Curl up one weight with a "one-two" count. Pause briefly. Lower and repeat with the other arm.

WELL-DEFINED CHEST...

Do the dumbbell fly. Lie on your back on a flat bench with your feet on the floor and an eight- to 10-pound dumbbell in each hand.

Slightly bend your arms, and place them directly out to your sides. Keep your palms up and the dumbbells in line with your chest. Let the dumbbells pull your arms down so you feel a slight stretch.

With an arcing motion, bring both the dumbbells together over your upper chest with your palms facing together. Slowly lower the dumbbells, and then repeat.

RIPPLING BACK...

Do a one-arm dumbbell row with the weights described for the biceps curl.

Lean over a flat bench, and place your left knee on the bench and your left hand at the top with your fingers curling over the side of the bench. Position yourself so your back is flat. Place your right foot securely on the floor. Hold a dumbbell in your right hand.

Fully extend your arm down with your palm facing your foot. Pull the dumbbell up to your hip, rotating your palm inward as you do so. Bring your elbow as far upward as you can. Slowly return to the starting position. Repeat on each side.

WASHBOARD STOMACH...

Do leg lifts. Lie on the floor on your back, and place your hands behind your head to elevate it. Lift your legs up to a 75° to 90° angle. Using your abdominal muscles, roll your buttocks off the floor, keeping your legs up.

Pull your elbows in toward your knees. Do not jerk your neck. Then slowly ease your buttocks back to the ground.

SIMPLER: If you can't lift your buttocks with your legs held up, do the exercise with your knees at a 45° angle.

FIRM BUTTOCKS...

Squats are the answer. Stand against a wall. Elevate your heels on a book (or books) two inches thick. Bend your knees and slide down until you reach a sitting position. Keep your back straight. Hold for a few seconds. Slowly come back up.

Squeeze your buttocks muscles as you return to the starting position. Don't lock your knees. Repeat.

STRONG THIGHS...

Do pliés—the ballet exercise. They'll also tone your abdominal muscles. Stand with your legs shoulder-width apart, toes pointed outward—what's known in ballet as second position.

Keeping your back, buttocks and hips aligned, bend your knees and go down as far as you can without lifting your heels off the floor. As soon as you reach the bottom of your plié, slowly return to the starting position. Squeeze your inner thighs as you raise your body.

SHAPELY LEGS...

Do walking lunges down a hallway or outside. Stand erect. Take a large step forward. Bend your knees and lower your body. Keep the knee of your forward leg above the ankle, and let the rear knee almost touch the floor.

Return to an upright position, and drag the trailing leg forward. Press the heel of your front leg down as you come up, and squeeze your buttocks together as your bring your legs back to the starting position.

Repeat on each leg.

DROP POUNDS FAST...

The basic fundamentals of weight loss never change. You must expend more calories than you consume. This becomes harder as you age because your metabolic rate slows.

BEST: Jump-start your day with at least 45 minutes of cardiovascular exercise (running, swimming, biking). You'll not only burn calories, you'll also work off some of your stored energy so it won't be converted to fat.

And...do strength-training exercises twice a week. As you build muscle, you'll raise your metabolic rate and burn more fat—even when you're resting—since muscle cells burn more calories than fat cells do.

IMPORTANT: Don't be lured by fad diets, such as the popular high-protein plans. The best way to lose pounds fast, safely and for good is to follow a diet high in fruits, vegetables and whole grains...and low in fat.

■

REPORT #46

BANISH YOUR BELLY FAT AT LAST!

Source: **Garry Egger, PhD, MPH,** director, Centre for Health Promotion and Research, Sydney, Australia, and adjunct professor of health sciences, Deakin University, Melbourne, Australia. He is coauthor of *GutBuster: Waist Loss Guide* (Allen & Unwin).

Whether it's called a potbelly or a spare tire, fat deposits concentrated around the middle of a man's body have long been the butt of jokes.

But mid-body fat is no laughing matter. It raises the risk for heart disease, diabetes, high blood pressure, back pain, knee problems, snoring and even impotence.

Almost every man develops at least a bit of a paunch as he grows older. How can you tell if yours is just a few harmless extra pounds or a reason for concern?

Do not rely on your bathroom scale—either to check yourself now or to monitor your weight loss later. A scale can tell you if you weigh more than most other men your height. But muscular men are sometimes overweight without being fat.

Your waist measurement is a more reliable indicator of potential health problems. Any man whose waist spans 39 inches or more should take immediate steps to lose his belly.

TO FIND YOUR WAIST SIZE: Place a tape measure around your waist at the level of the navel. Do not suck in your gut. That will only give you an artificially small number—reassuring, perhaps, but dangerously misleading.

SIX WAYS TO SHRINK A BELLY...

The good news for men is that it's not especially difficult to lose a potbelly. Abdominal fat tends to be more "mobile" than weight that is deposited at the hips and thighs—as women's fat often is.

Follow these guidelines, and you should lose an inch of fat in your waist measurement every two to three weeks...

1. *Cut fat consumption dramatically.* Most health experts continue to recommend getting about 30% of total calories in the form of fat. But it's not really the percentage of dietary fat that counts. It's the total amount of fat that you eat that controls how fat your body is.

IMPORTANT: Eat no more than 40 grams (g) of fat per day. Pick up a fat-count book, like Karen J. Bellerson's *The Complete & Up-to-Date Fat Book* (Avery).

Recent research suggests that dietary fat is actually addictive—the more you eat, the more you crave. Stop eating fatty foods for just two weeks, and you should lose most, if not all, of your craving.

2. *Eat small, frequent meals.* Doing so boosts your metabolic rate, speeding the rate at which the body burns calories and helping you avoid the hunger that sometimes leads to uncontrolled eating. Never go more than four hours without eating. Do *not* skip breakfast. If you have no appetite upon rising, start the day with toast and juice.

3. *Focus simply on moving more*—not necessarily getting more exercise. Vigorous exercise is unnecessary. Your goal should be simply to boost the amount of time you spend in motion—going up stairs, walking the dog, mowing the lawn, etc.

Stomach exercises do firm the abdominal muscles. But they have no special magic against belly fat. Walking is actually more effective, since it's a more efficient way of burning calories.

4. *Cultivate a caffeine habit.* Too much coffee or any other caffeinated beverage can cause health problems, including anxiety. But it's now clear that a little caffeine each day constitutes a safe way to speed your metabolism and lose weight.

Because the body quickly develops a tolerance to caffeine, drinking coffee, cola, etc., is most effective after a period of abstinence.

If you're a habitual coffee, tea or cola drinker, go "cold turkey." After two weeks, gradually reintroduce caffeine into your diet. Limit consumption to two cups of coffee—or four cups of tea or cola—per day.

If you're not much of a caffeinated beverage drinker right now, start slowly. Have one-half cup of coffee in the morning and one-half cup in the afternoon.

5. *Season your food with hot peppers. Capsaicin,* the compound that makes hot peppers hot, fights body fat in two ways. It increases your metabolism...and helps reduce the amount of food eaten at each meal. It does the latter by curbing your appetite.

SOURCES OF CAPSAICIN: Red and green chili peppers, cayenne pepper, Tabasco sauce and jalapeños.

6. *Observe your drinking habits.* Contrary to popular belief, alcohol is not a significant contributor to a potbelly. It's the chips, cheese, etc., that you eat while drinking alcohol that add on the pounds.

■

REPORT #47

CURE BALDNESS NATURALLY

Source: **Jeanette Jacknin, MD,** board-certified dermatologist and member of the medical advisory board of the Physicians Skin Institute in Scottsdale, AZ.

The average adult scalp contains an estimated 100,000 hair follicles and loses approximately 100 hairs a day. Normally, they're replaced in five or six weeks. New hair sprouts out of tiny, tube-shaped follicles in the scalp.

The most common type of hair loss is *androgenic alopecia.* This male (or female) pattern hair loss causes hair to grow back thinner (less hair on the scalp) or finer (each individual hair is thinner). Or it doesn't grow back at all.

How can you slow, stop or even reverse hair loss? *Minoxidil* (Rogaine), a topical treatment for men and women, is available in both prescription and over-the-counter (OTC) strengths. It is believed to work by affecting potassium-regulating mechanisms in the hair follicle. Dermatologists who prescribe minoxidil typically find that one-third of patients using it have some new hair growth...one-third find their hair loss slows or stops...and one-third do not have any improvement. It can cause a rash on your scalp, costs $50 a month and must be used indefinitely.

Men can take the oral prescription medication *finasteride* (Propecia), a synthetic hormone that blocks the formation of DHT. But this drug can inhibit erections and sex drive.

In addition, there are hundreds of OTC treatments which promise—but fail to deliver—miraculous results.

NATURAL TREATMENTS...

Several natural hair-loss remedies have been shown to be effective—without causing side effects...

• *Saw palmetto.* This is the number-one herbal treatment of choice for androgenic alopecia in men. It works just like finasteride, blocking the formation of *5-alpha reductase,* an enzyme that sparks the conversion of testosterone to DHT. But saw palmetto doesn't have the same side effects as finasteride. In fact, it may enhance sexual function. It can cause increased appetite and breast enlargement.

TYPICAL DOSE: 160 milligrams (mg) daily.

SCIENTIFIC EVIDENCE: In research reported in the April 2002 issue of the *Journal of Alternative and Complementary Medicine,* 19 men between the ages of 23 and 64 with mild to moderate androgenic alopecia were given either saw palmetto or a placebo for five months. Of those who took the herb, 60% reported a slower rate of hair loss, more hair growth, a smaller bald spot and/or higher satisfaction with the appearance of their hair. Of those getting the placebo, only 11% reported any improvement.

• *Procyanidin B-3.* A number of studies conducted in Japan show that procyanidin—a type of flavonoid (plant pigment) extracted from barley—promotes hair growth.

SCIENTIFIC EVIDENCE: In a laboratory study published in the December 2002 issue of *Experimental Dermatology,* researchers tested more than 1,000 plant extracts to discover which best promoted the growth of hair cells. The scientists found that procyanidin B-3 outperformed the control group by 140%. Procyanidin also was found to have no side effects.

HELPFUL: The topical hair-loss product Revivogen, for men and women, contains both saw palmetto and procyanidin. To order, call 888-616-4247 or go to *www.revivogen.com.* Crinagen, a topical spray for men, also contains both natural extracts. To order, call 877-298-0128 or go to *www.raztec.com.*

OTHER TYPES OF HAIR LOSS...

Androgenic alopecia isn't the only cause of hair loss. Thyroid disease, severe stress and side effects of medication also can lead to hair loss. In some cases, an inflammatory condition can strip the scalp of hair. Examples include irritant dermatitis (a skin reaction to a chemical in a hair product such as shampoo) and alopecia areata (an autoimmune skin disease).

To combat hair loss associated with inflammation, ask your doctor about taking a daily supplement of 500 mg of gamma-linolenic acid (GLA), an anti-inflammatory essential fatty acid found naturally in the seeds of evening primrose, black currant and borage plants.

IMPORTANT: GLA should not be taken by women who are pregnant or nursing. Because GLA has anticlotting effects, people taking *warfarin* (Coumadin) or other blood thinners, as well as hemophiliacs, should consult their doctors before taking it.

AROMATHERAPY...

The "essential oils" of aromatherapy can increase blood flow to the scalp, which helps promote hair regrowth.

WHAT TO DO: In a small, clean bottle, add one to two drops of essential oil of cayenne for each ounce of essential oil of rosemary. Use only enough of the mixture to lightly coat your scalp, and massage into your scalp for 20 minutes daily. Use any shampoo to rinse.

■

REPORT #48

QUICK FIXES FOR ACHING FEET!

Source: **Suzanne M. Levine, DPM**, podiatrist in private practice in New York City. She is author of *Your Feet Don't Have to Hurt* (St. Martin's).

Anyone who has ever suffered from athlete's foot knows that antifungal creams usually clear up the condition in about two weeks. What most people don't know is that the medication must be used for a full month to eradicate the fungus.

Like athlete's foot, most foot problems are either caused—or worsened—by the sufferers themselves. **HERE ARE FIVE PAINFUL FOOT AILMENTS AND THE MISTAKES THAT CAUSE THEM...**

BUNIONS...

Millions of American adults undergo surgery each year to remove bunions—bony protrusions on the outside of the big toe. Many of these surgeries could be prevented with self-care.

COMMON MISTAKE: Wearing high heels or shoes with tight toes. This can cause inflammation and swelling, which irritate and worsen the bunions. To avoid this problem, it's important to buy shoes that are not too tight in the toe box.

If you already suffer from bunions, you can reduce the pressure with over-the-counter (OTC) orthotic inserts that support the arch. If they don't help, you may need to get prescription orthotics from a podiatrist.

TYPICAL COST: $250 to $500.

Wearing snug socks also reduces the friction on bunions.

TO RELIEVE PAINFUL BUNION ATTACKS: Mix up one cup of vinegar in one gallon of warm water, and soak the foot for 15 minutes daily. Also, wrap ice or a package of frozen peas in a thin towel and apply to the bunion twice a day for 15 minutes. These treatments will reduce swelling and pain.

CALLUSES...

Calluses are thick layers of dead skin cells that accumulate in areas of the foot exposed to frequent pressure. High heels or flat shoes can make calluses worse by shifting body weight to the forefoot. Shoes with one-inch heels are preferable because they put less pressure on this part of the foot.

COMMON MISTAKE: Using the OTC callus-removal products. They don't always work well—and the active ingredient (*salicylic acid*) can damage healthy skin. It is also often more effective to remove calluses after taking a warm bath or shower.

WHAT TO DO: Very gently abrade the callus with a pumice stone. Before going to bed, apply a moisturizer that contains copper, a softening agent that will make calluses easier to remove.

If this process doesn't help, ask your doctor about *microdermabrasion*. This 15- to 30-minute, painless outpatient procedure eliminates the need for surgery. During microdermabrasion, a podiatrist uses aluminum oxide crystals to exfoliate the callus.

TYPICAL COST: $125 to $200.

CORNS...

These kernel-shaped areas of thickened tissue are similar to calluses but usually form at the tips of—or between—toes.

COMMON MISTAKE: Cutting or roughly abrading corns. This causes more pain and often results in infection. It's more effective to soak the corn in an Epsom salt solution for 10 minutes. Then gently rub the corn with a pumice stone. Repeat the treatment daily until the corn is gone.

FALLEN ARCHES...

People develop fallen arches when the feet flatten over time. This happens when aging, weight gain, excess impact from running or walking and/or hormonal changes cause loosening of the *plantar fascia* ligaments at the bottom of the feet. Other people may have inherited a low arch. The condition triggers arch pain—often accompanied by heel or ankle pain.

COMMON MISTAKE: Forgoing physical activity. Inactivity usually worsens the condition. Arch pain can usually be reduced or eliminated with exercises that stretch the Achilles tendons and strengthen the muscles of the arch.

Do each of the following stretches six times, twice daily. Hold each stretch for 30 seconds.

• *Place your right foot on a chair or step.* Keep both heels flat. Lean forward over the chair or step until you feel a stretch in the right calf. Repeat with the left foot.

• *Stand on a step facing the stairs with your feet together.* Move your right heel back until it hangs off the edge. Lower the heel until you feel a stretch in the right calf. Repeat with the left foot.

• *Sit in a chair.* Rest your right ankle on your left knee. Gently pull the toes of your right foot upward toward your chest, until you feel a stretch in the arch of the foot. Repeat with the left foot.

People with fallen arches should wear dress shoes with one-inch heels or athletic shoes with built-in arches. Slip-in orthotic inserts (either prescription or OTC) are helpful for restoring proper arch and support.

TO DETERMINE IF YOU HAVE FALLEN ARCHES: Walk in wet sand, and look at your footprints. The print of a normal foot has a gap between the heel and the forefoot. However, a fallen arch will have little or no gap.

INGROWN NAILS...

Ingrown toenails curve and push into the flesh instead of growing straight over the toe. The condition causes pain, redness and/or swelling at the ends or sides of the toes.

COMMON MISTAKE: Trimming nails on a curve. That increases the risk for ingrown nails. To reduce this risk, soak your feet in warm water, wash thoroughly with soap and trim the nails straight across.

If there is redness or other signs of infection, apply an OTC antibiotic, such as Neosporin.

IF PAIN AND REDNESS DO NOT GO AWAY AFTER TWO DAYS: Your doctor may need to remove the portion of nail beneath the skin. This can be done in a 15-minute outpatient procedure.

■

REPORT #49

EAT NO WHITE AT NIGHT, THE WORLD'S EASIEST DIET

Source: **Bill Gavin, MD,** cardiologist and director of the Heart Program at St. Peter Hospital in Olympia, WA. Dr. Gavin is also the author of *No White at Night: The Three-Rule Diet* (Riverhead).

Nearly everyone who starts a new diet loses weight initially. But, up to 95% of these dieters fail to maintain their weight loss after one year. And, some people gain back even *more* pounds than they lost. Most diets are too complex or restrictive to stick with for very long. People get frustrated.

The basic diet that works best for my patients—one that's recommended by the prestigious Institute of Medicine—consists of 40% carbohydrates, 30% protein and 30% fat. You do not need to be exact—just checking food labels will keep you in the target zone. Over the past five years, hundreds of patients who followed my basic diet program lost an average of one pound every one to two weeks, and a majority of these patients sustained their weight loss for a year.

MY STORY: When I hit 210 pounds at age 46, I had to get serious about losing weight. I exercised almost fanatically at first, but lost only about 10 pounds in six months, since I did not change my diet. When I started researching and implementing commonsense dietary principles, I lost 35 additional pounds.

Based on my experience, I developed three basic rules for weight loss and wrote them on prescription blanks for patients who found popular diet plans too complicated...

RULE #1: EAT THREE MEALS A DAY...

Approximately 70% of people who end up in weight-loss programs have never made a habit of eating breakfast, and many skip lunch as well. Therefore, they're ravenous by 5 pm and often consume more calories at dinner than they would if they ate three sensible daily meals.

Dinner is the largest meal for most Americans, which is opposite of what you need for weight loss. In laboratory studies, rats that consume most of their calories at night do gain more weight than animals who are given an equal number of calories spread throughout the day.

It is acceptable to distribute all your calories equally at each meal, but you'll lose weight more efficiently if you get most of your calories at breakfast and lunch and fewer at dinner.

HELPFUL: Do not eat anything within three hours of going to sleep, when your body's metabolism is slowest. Calories at that time have a greater tendency to go into storage.

RULE #2: EAT LEAN PROTEIN WITH EVERY MEAL...

It curbs hunger more effectively than fat or carbohydrates.

TRY THIS: On one morning, have a bagel for breakfast and slather it with all the jam you want. Write down how many hours after breakfast you get hungry. The next day, eat another bagel topped with two tablespoons of natural peanut butter. You will discover that you do not get hungry for an additional two hours because of the protein in the peanut butter.

Eat at least 10 to 15 grams (g) of protein with each meal. That is roughly the amount in three egg whites...two tablespoons of natural peanut butter...one-half-cup of nonfat cottage cheese...or one-and-a-half ounces of turkey. This is the minimum amount that is needed to curb hunger. The average person requires more overall—about 1 g of protein daily for every two pounds of body weight.

SELF-TEST: If you're hungry one to two hours after eating, you probably need more protein.

RULE #3: EAT NO WHITE AT NIGHT...

This means no white rice, bread, potatoes or pasta at your evening meal. You'll also want to avoid red potatoes, brown rice, whole-wheat bread and starchy vegetables, such as corn and peas. At dinner have lean meat, fish or poultry, and all the salad and nonstarchy vegetables you want.

The "white" carbohydrates tend to have a high glycemic index, a measurement of how fast blood sugar rises after eating. Foods with a high glycemic index produce a high insulin response. They can increase your blood sugar about 90% as fast as pure sugar.

The increased insulin response causes your blood sugar to decrease rapidly, which in turn causes more hunger. Eating these high-glycemic foods at night causes higher insulin in the day. This almost guarantees weight gain.

During the initial few months of your diet, you might want to give up white, starchy foods altogether. Once you have reached your target weight, you can reintroduce them into your diet —but never at night.

SELF-TEST: If your energy slumps within one to two hours after eating, you've probably had too many carbohydrates.

DR. GAVIN'S OTHER SECRETS...

To lose weight more quickly, also do the following...
- *Drink at least one-and-a-half to two quarts of water daily.*
- *Exercise at least 30 minutes seven days a week.*

■

REPORTS #50

THE CURE FOR OLD AGE

Source: **Bradley J. Willcox, MD**, physician-investigator in geriatrics, Pacific Health Research Institute, and assistant professor of geriatrics, University of Hawaii, both in Honolulu.

The residents of Okinawa, a chain of islands in Japan, are among the healthiest and longest-lived people in the world. Okinawa has more 100-year-olds than anywhere else—33.6 per 100,000 people, compared with approximately 10 per 100,000 in the United States.

The 25-year Okinawa Centenarian Study discovered that, compared with Americans, Okinawans have...

- *80% lower risk of breast and prostate cancers.*
- *50% lower risk of colon and ovarian cancers.*
- *40% fewer hip fractures.*
- *Minimal risk of heart disease.*

What's the secret to the Okinawans' longevity—and what can we do to achieve the same healthful vigor? **THE FOLLOWING FACTORS ARE ESPECIALLY IMPORTANT...**

ACCEPTING ATTITUDE...

While many Americans have Type A personalities, Okinawans believe that life's travails will work themselves out. The average American might be said to suffer from *hurry sickness.* But Okinawans prefer to work at their own pace, which is referred to locally as *Okinawa Time.* They don't ignore stress...but they rarely internalize it. Stress signals your body to secrete large amounts of *cortisol* and other stress hormones. That damages the heart and blood vessels and accelerates bone loss.

TO REDUCE STRESS: Don't take on more than you can handle...take advantage of flextime at work...don't get worked up about things you can't change, such as traffic jams or rude behavior...practice deep breathing and meditation.

LOW-CALORIE INTAKE...

Okinawans consume an average of 1,900 calories a day, compared with 2,500 for Americans. Studies have shown that